Italian edition © 2003 «L'ERMA» di BRETSCHNEIDER

First published in the United States of America
in 2003 by
Getty Publications
1200 Getty Center Drive, Suite 500
Los Angeles, California 90049-1682
www.getty.edu

English translation © 2003 J. Paul Getty Trust

Christopher Hudson, *Publisher*
Mark Greenberg, *Editor in Chief*
Eriksen Translations, Inc., *Translator*
Robin H. Ray, *Copy Editor*
Agnes Anderson, *Cover Designer*

Giovanni Portieri, *Graphic Designer*
Maurizio Pinto, *Computer Layout and Pagination*

F. Esposito, A. De Carolis, E. De Carolis, *Photographic Archive*
Typeset and printed in Italy
by «L'ERMA» di BRETSCHNEIDER

Library of Congress Cataloging-in-Publication Data

De Carolis, Ernesto.
Vesuvius, A.D. 79 : the destruction of Pompeii and Herculaneum / Ernesto
De Carolis, Giovanni Patricelli.
p. cm.
Includes bibliographical references.
ISBN 0-89236-719-9 (pbk.)
1. Vesuvius (Italy) – Eruption, 79 2. Pompeii (Extinct city) 3. Herculaneum
(Extinct city) 4. Excavations (Archaeology) – Italy – Pompeii (Extinct city)
5. Excavations (Archaeology) – Italy – Herculaneum (Extinct city)
6. Italy – Antiquities. I. Patricelli, Giovanni. II. Title
DG70.P7D3722003
937'.7– dc21
2002156657

On the front cover:
View of the great eruption of Mount Vesuvius on Sunday night,
August the 8th, 1779. Hand-colored etching from William Hamilton,
Supplement to the Campi Phlegraei, Naples, 1779,
pl. 2. Los Angeles, Getty Research Institute, 84-B27609

On the back cover:
The 1631 eruption of Vesuvius, with the procession of the relics
of San Gennaro (Micco Spadaro, 1609-1675). Oil on canvas.
Frontispiece:
P.J. Volaire (1729-1802), *The Eruption of Vesuvius.* Oil on canvas.

Photographic credits:
Archaeological Superintendence of Pompeii:
19, 38, 40, 51, 53, 56, 58, 72, 73, 92, 105
Archaeological Superintendence of Naples and Caserta:
33, 35, 52, 54, 55, 59
Special Superintendence for the Museums of Naples:
Frontispiece, 21

Table of Contents

Preface

Why is the A.D. 79 eruption of Vesuvius so unique? It is not the largest explosive volcanic event in history, nor is it the one that caused the largest number of fatalities. That dubious distinction must go to the great Tambora eruption in Indonesia in 1815. The Vesuvius eruption is unique because no other eruption in history has had such a profound effect on our culture and also illustrated to us the terror and destruction of an awesome and sublime natural catastrophe. When Vesuvius erupted in A.D. 79, it accomplished a number of things. It caused a regional disaster that took thousands of lives and buried the two major Roman cities of Pompeii and Herculaneum beneath a hot blanket of ash and pumice to such a depth that they were not inhabited again for a millennium. It is not only the magnitude of the disaster that is so compelling, but equally its completeness in interring such a large region and a population that represents a complete cross-section of Roman society of its time. No other active volcano has erupted within such a densely populated region. As a result of the disaster, Rome lost one of its greatest scholars, Pliny the Elder, who gave his life in an attempt to study the natural disaster. But emerging from the devastation of the eruption came Pliny the Younger, first as chronicler of the disaster and of his uncle's death, who later became an important civil servant. His unique account is the first eyewitness report of a volcanic eruption as well as a historic landmark that signals the beginning of the study of volcanoes.

However, the most important cultural impact of the eruption of Vesuvius began to emerge when the cities were rediscovered in the eighteenth century. The lethal blanket of volcanic ash and pumice had preserved in the ground a time capsule of the art, architecture, and culture of an entire civilization, in a state of completeness and detail like at no other archaeological site on Earth. The resulting process of discovery in Herculaneum

The Children of Joachim Murat visiting the theater at Herculaneum (N. Lemasle, 1789-1870, oil on canvas)

and Pompeii simply demanded the creation of new disciplines, and thus the unearthing of the cities led to the emergence of both archaeology and of art history as new and important endeavours of human culture. When images of the unearthed sculptures, art, and objects began to circulate throughout Europe, they led to a rejuvenation of interest in the classical and the birth of the neo-classical style. The drama of the catastrophic event called forth a widespread response in literature and art, seeking to display the last days of Pompeii. As volcanology developed from a largely descriptive endeavour in the nineteenth century to a more quantitative science in the latter part of the twentieth century, an understanding of the processes associated with a major explosive eruption began to emerge. The early and simplistic views that the cities of Vesuvius were buried rapidly by an intense rain of ashes and mudflows gradually gave way to more complex models. As so often happens in science, it is the observation of a current event that gives us the key or the clues to the understanding of the past. The first breakthrough in the study of the Vesuvius eruption occurred in the aftermath of the 1902 eruption of Montagne Pelee in Martinique in the West Indies, when the devastation of pyroclastic surges and pyroclastic flows was dramatically brought home. Our thorough accounting of the natural disaster of A.D. 79 was not possible, however, until the experience of the eruptions of Mount St. Helens in the USA in 1980 and El Chichon in Mexico in 1982 provided the guiding light in interpreting the volcanic deposits in Pompeii and Herculaneum and integrating the stratigraphic record with the faithful account of Pliny the Younger.

What have we learned from this terrible disaster? We know that Vesuvius is active, and that it has a long history of catastrophic eruptions of this magnitude that have occurred repeatedly throughout its lifetime of seventeen thousand years. Have we learned to live with the sleeeping giant? Judging from the current urban sprawl and the rapid commercial and residential development that is creeping up the slopes of the volcano, I must sadly conclude that we have not yet learned the lesson.

Haraldur Sigurdsson
University of Rhode Island, USA

Introduction

After centuries of repose, *Vesuvius Mons* awoke. On the morning of August 24, in the year A.D. 79, the inhabitants of the area around Vesuvius were astonished by sinister rumbling and the first explosions that came from the familiar mountain, the slopes of which were covered with vineyards and luxuriant woods. Then the roar of a thousand claps of thunder spread across the area while the earth trembled, throwing people, animals, and objects off balance. Then came a continuous, dense rain of pumice that covered and whitened both city and countryside. Then the hot cloud of cinders that overwhelmed everything in its path and then... In 1710, while digging a well in Herculaneum, a worker accidentally hit a finely polished block of marble. Thus began the long and laborious discovery of the cities destroyed by the volcano's fury, engendering a florescence of study and research as well as a continuous pilgrimage of visitors and curiosity seekers, lured by the possibility of wandering amid streets, houses, workshops, and sacred and public buildings that were once full of life and echoed with the voices of their inhabitants. The enthusiasm and fascination inspired by the cities buried in ash on that hot late August day have been the basis for innumerable works that have attempted, with varying degrees of success, to reconstruct and understand the world of the ancient Vesuvians, up to their last moments of life. The disaster has been approached through fantasy and realism, imagination and precise documentation, poetry and science. With this publication, our goal, which we have hopefully achieved, has been to describe as exhaustively as possible the terrible event that lies behind the immortal fame of the Vesuvian cities.

Thus we have brought together the most recent volcanological and archaeological data with a series of concepts that are simple and easily understood, but not imprecise. The result is a description of the territory around Vesuvius, the impact of human settlement there, and the rapid succession of eruptions that disturbed the entire area, particularly Pompeii and Herculaneum.

As a natural introduction to the main body of the book, we have included information on volcanic activity in general and on the different types of eruptions, with a glossary of scientific terms. Particular attention has been paid to the story of the volcanic complex of Somma-Vesuvius. Finally, the last part of the book deals with the interest and emotions aroused by the unearthing of human bodies in the complex history of Pompeii's discovery.

Reconstructing the Vesuvian area in the first century A.D. is particularly complex, even today, because of two factors: the continuous eruptions that have occurred over the centuries, beginning with the famous one of A.D. 79, and the intense urbanization of the entire region, which has accelerated in recent decades. To varying degrees, these factors have profoundly altered the appearance of the area without, however, producing effects as profound as those following the A.D. 79 eruption. That event resulted in the mass exodus of those who survived the terrifying event, the obliteration, albeit temporary, of the territory's productive life, and change to the coastline and the course of the Sarno River, a vital artery for the economy of this part of Campania. With the help of ancient sources and continued interdisciplinary research, we now possess a great quantity of data, the collation of which has allowed us to attempt a reconstruction of the geological, urban, and productive

appearance of the area of Vesuvius in the first century A.D. The territory that was the backdrop for the catastrophic eruption consisted of the area between the city of Herculaneum and the site of Stabiae along the coastline, the slopes of Vesuvius and the Lattari mountain chain, with penetration inland into the substantially flat area characterized by the winding path of the Sarno river. Specifically the city of Herculaneum and the suburban Villa of the Papyri, separated by a stream-filled ravine, faced directly toward the sea, from a strongly elevated position. Pompeii, in contrast, built on a high lava spur, stood in the immediate vicinity of the Vesuvian coast, which was lined with the residential villas of wealthy Roman society, as well as sheltering various coastal settlements.

On the other hand, the inland countryside was characterized by rustic villas of varying sizes, depending on the size of the property. Plots were used for various types of crops and livestock. The slopes of Vesuvius and the Lattari Mountains had extensive vineyards and, toward the summit, large areas forested with oak and beech trees that the inhabitants of the area used for wood.

The connections between the urban settlements and the villas were assured by a well-developed road network, both local and connecting to neighboring Naples and Nuceria.

Somma-Vesuvius

The Campanian Plain

The volcanic areas that are active today (Vesuvius, the Phlegraean Fields, and Ischia) are located in a broad, low area known as the Campanian Plain, southeast of the Lattari Mountains on the Sorrentine Peninsula, north and northeast of the Caserti Mountains and the western edge of the Picentine Mountains, and finally northwest of Monte Massico. The Campanian Plain (fig. 1) was formed in the late Pliocene era (approximately two million years ago), along the western edge of the Apennine chain, following the general sinking of the calcareous lands that extended continuously from the Sorrentine Peninsula to Monte Massico. The lowering of this area is the result of tectonic movements that led to the formation of the Tyrrhenian basin, begun approximately seven million years ago. This movement,

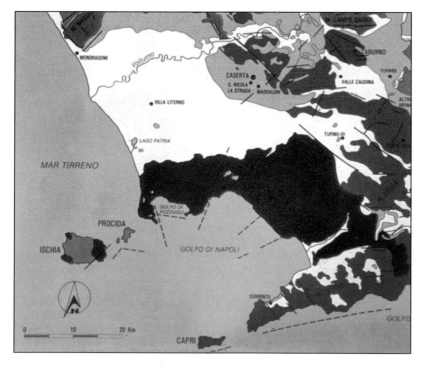

1. Structural-geological scheme of the area of Campania, showing the Neapolitan volcanic zone, indicated in red, within the Campanian Plain, in yellow, bordered by the mountain chains mentioned in the text, in green and blue (from *La Ricerca Scientifica* 114, 8, 1987).

2. Development of the eruptive column of La Soufrière volcano, on the island of Montserrat, which resumed activity in 1995.

still in progress today, rotates toward the eastern part of the Italian peninsula.

The enormous forces that caused the depression of this area created deep faults in the crust of the earth. These faults facilitated the rise of magmatic fluids and resulted in the formation of the volcanic structures found along the Tyrrhenian coast. In fact, much of the volcanic activity in Campania is located along the fault systems that originated within the context of these processes.

VOLCANIC ACTIVITY

Volcanic activity is the surface manifestation of processes that take place within the earth's crust and the underlying mantle. Rising magma (fluids of siliceous composition created by the fusion of rocks) accumulates in specific areas of the earth's crust, called magmatic chambers, which are generally located at a depth of 1 to 10 kilometers. Here the magma ceases to flow but develops chemically as it waits to begin the final stage of its journey to the surface.

In conduits that link the magmatic chamber to the earth's surface, and along which the magma tends to rise, phenomena occur that will determine an eruption's degree of explosiveness and danger. The composition of the magma and the percentage of volatile substances (gas and especially water) dissolved in it will influence the volcano's future course of action. In terms of volcanic activity, the dominating process is the degassing that the magma undergoes in areas closest to the surface, with the liberation of volatile substances that were found in solution in the deepest area of the magmatic column. The solubility of water and gases contained in the magmatic liquids increases with the growth of confining pressure and is dependent on the chemical composition of the magma as well as on its temperature.

As the magma rises toward the surface, confining pressure diminishes, causing a decrease in the solubility of the volatiles. Gas bubbles, also called vesicles, begin to form within the magma. The continuous, gradual decrease in pressure as the magma rises causes constant expansion and aggregation of the gas bubbles, which shift upward in the magmatic column, since their density is lower than that of the liquid. Vesiculation, enabling the growth and rise of the bubbles, is strongly affected by the viscosity of the magma, depending on its pressure, temperature, and composition.

In basic magma, with generally low viscosity, the gases released are able to escape with relative ease, generally resulting in effusive or flowing eruptions. With acidic and more viscous magma, the liberation of gases occurs with greater difficulty. The pressure within the vesicles increases until it overcomes the opposing resistance of the liquid and explodes, launching shreds of liquid magma and solid fragments of the conduit into the air. The resulting eruptions are of an explosive nature (fig. 2).

Effusive Eruptions

These eruptions, classified as Strombolian or Hawaiian in type, are characterized by a low level of explosiveness. They are caused by basic magma that is relatively low in gas, high in temperature (1200 °F), and low in viscosity.

In these types of eruptions, the bubbles formed through vesiculation rise more easily within the magmatic column and do not build up pressure, due to the low resistance that the magma offers.

In Strombolian eruptions (normal for the Stromboli volcano on the Italian island of the same name, in the Aeolian archipelago), which

3. Fountain of lava on Etna during the eruption of December 1985.

are moderately explosive, generally the expansion and aggregation of bubbles creates a single large vesicle that explodes once it arrives at the surface. In doing so, it emits fragments of magma, which, as they rapidly cool down, form so-called scoria, blobs of frozen lava pitted with holes. The emission of larger fragments creates veritable bombs.

Eruptions of the Hawaiian type (characteristic of the volcanoes in the archipelago of Hawaii) are characterized by moderate emissions of basic magma, with smaller explosions and little ash or lava shards.

The flow is particularly high in such cases. Spectacular fountains of lava form (fig. 3), which can reach heights of hundreds of meters, when a portion of the magma reaches the surface, flowing slowly along the sides of the volcano and creating large streams of lava.

4. Eruptive column that developed during the eruption of Pinatubo, the Philippines, June 1991.

5. Eruptive column that developed during the eruption of Mount St. Helens in May 1980.

Plinian Explosive Eruptions

In acidic magma, the expansion, aggregation, and rise of bubbles create at the surface of the magmatic column a sort of foam, made up of magma and bubbles. The process tends to cease when the bubbles become closely packed and the viscosity of the magma prevents further expansion. At that point the pressure of the gases inside the vesicles increases until it exceeds the force of the magma's cohesion. With the explosion of the bubbles, fragmentation begins, generally at the depth of some hundreds of meters. The magma is reduced to minute particles (ash) and shards that, by cooling rapidly, preserve gas bubbles in their internal cavities. The resulting rock is called pumice.

Thus a low viscosity mix is formed, made up of fine particles of magma and gas, which is accelerated through the conduit. Its velocity, on the order of one to several hundred meters per second, depends on its physical properties and on the dimensions and form of the conduit. The emission of this mixture from the volcanic conduit forms a violent, high-velocity jet of gas filled with pumice and ash. It mixes turbulently with the surrounding air, heating it and causing it to form an eruptive cloud, dense with ash and pyroclastic fragments. This cloud, being lighter than the surrounding air, rises to a height of some scores of kilometers (as high as 50 or 60 kilometers, depending on the quantity of thermal energy transmitted into the atmosphere) (fig. 4). Continuous mixing with the air decreases the temperature of the eruptive column. Eventually it reaches a level at which its pressure is depleted and the densities of the clouds and the atmosphere fall back into balance. This is the point of the greatest lateral expansion of the cloud in the direction of the stratospheric winds, and the lightest materials, such as pumice and ash, are transported for distances up to hundreds of kilometers. The heavier materials, such as the volcanic bombs, tend to fall according to ballistic trajectories (fig. 5). Over the course of eruptions of this type (defined as Plinian in honor of Pliny the Elder, the Roman naturalist who died in the eruption of Vesuvius in A.D. 79), which are violently

6. The collapse of an eruptive column originates from pyroclastic flows of high temperature and velocity that are distributed along the sides of a volcano. The photo shows a pyroclastic cloud flowing down the side of Mount St. Helens during the eruption of August 7, 1980.

explosive in nature, volcanoes can emit great volumes of pyroclastic material, made up of pumice, lapilli (pebble-sized stones), various lithic stones, and large fragments. Sometimes the ascent of the eruptive column is incomplete, or the column may collapse, when the quantity of energy suffusing the air is insufficient to create a mix that has lower density than air. This collapse can result from an expansion of the eruptive mouth, an increase in the mass of materials emitted, or a reduced velocity of the mix due to a lesser concentration of gases and therefore less pressure.

The collapse of the eruptive column creates pyroclastic flows (fig. 6), surging superheated clouds (with temperatures up to 300–400 °C) made up of gases and liquid magma fragments that literally roll down the sides of the volcano, reaching speeds of sometimes more than 100 kilometers per hour and arriving at distances up to scores of kilometers from the eruptive center. The enormous destructive potential of these flows makes them the most dangerous events associated with explosive eruptions (fig. 7).

Pyroclastic Materials of Explosive Eruptions

The materials emitted during the explosive activity of a volcano are called pyroclastic materials, shards of magma that, expelled from the vent, cool down and accumulate, forming pyroclastic rocks. Most of these materials are vitreous (glassy) in nature, since during the magma's rise in the volcanic conduit, the expansion of gases causes rapid cooling that prevents crystals from forming.
Thus we have the formation of pumice, white-gray in color, and scoriae, dark red. Both are characterized by a vesicular structure, with a network of cavities left by the expulsion of gases. These holes are more numerous in pumice, making it very light. In addition to the materials that are defined as vitreous, various lithic fragments can be emitted in a solid state. These are categorized as follows:

a. Juvenile fragments, produced directly by the cooling of the magma; these can be partially

7. A spectacular shot of the surge during the eruption of Mount St. Helens in May 1980 (photo M. Moore).

crystallized, depending on the degree of development before the eruption.

b. Accessory lithic stones, solid fragments deposited in the volcanic conduit by earlier eruptions, which are later expelled.

c. Accidental lithic stones, coming from the base of the structure; these can be non-volcanic in origin, such as the calcareous fragments present in the materials expelled from Vesuvius.

Pyroclastic materials, depending on their size, can be categorized as:

a. bombs and blocks, with dimensions larger than 64 mm;

b. lapilli, with dimensions from 2 to 64 mm;

c. ash, with dimensions less than 2 mm.

The so-called accretional (pisolitic) lapilli are particularly noteworthy. These are formed by the concentric growth of ash around a core of condensation. They are present in eruptions that are rich in water, which create suspended ash clouds and often indicate events of a hydro-magmatic nature.

8. Schematic diagram of the various eruptive phenomena.

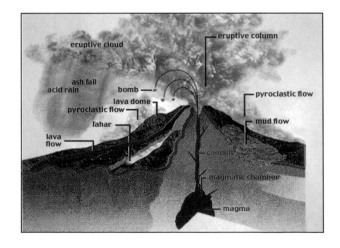

9. Phreatic explosion at Mount St. Helens (USA), in April 1980, preceding the principal violent event of May 18.

The modes of emission of these materials can be summarized in three typologies (fig. 8):

a. deposits from the fallout phase, directly from the Plinian cloud, in which the largest pieces fall around the point of emission following ballistic trajectories, while the finer materials are carried by stratospheric winds to more distant areas;

b. deposits from pyroclastic flows, clouds of material with higher percentages of solid particles than gases, which pour down the sides of the volcano, running into pre-existing valley depressions;

c. deposits from pyroclastic surges, clouds of material at high velocity and temperature, richer in gases than in solid particles.

Often pyroclastic surges and flows can originate from the same superheated cloud; in this case the surge, being more fluid, precedes the flow in running along the terrain. Lahars are another phenomenon tied to explosive eruptions. These are avalanches of mud that occur when great quantities of ash that have accumulated on the slopes of the volcano are saturated by rain and steam emitted during the volcanic activity and then remobilize. In this way a huge volume of material can be transported downhill, flowing along depressions in the terrain.

Phreatomagmatic Eruptions and Phreatic Explosions

Eruptive manifestations in which the magma interacts with ground- or seawater are called phreatic. In phreatic explosions the magma encounters an aquifer on its way to the surface. It gives off part of its heat to the water,

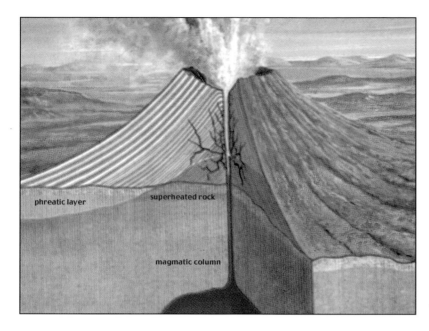

Labels in image: phreatic layer, superheated rock, magmatic column

10. Schematic drawing of phreatomagmatic activity (drawing by L. K. Townsend).

raising the temperature and causing evaporation. Enormous pressure is thus created causing steam and water flows that are thrust toward the less resistant rock zones. When the overlying rocks are not fractured instantaneously, no eruption occurs. But if the pressure generated is greater than that imposed by the contiguous rocks, and if the steam can spread inside, then the rocks do fracture, resulting in a phreatic eruptive phase in which steam and fragments of covering rock are expelled. In a phreatic explosion the magma also may not reach the surface if its energy is insufficient. In this type of situation columns of steam several kilometers high may form, with large masses expelled for hundreds of meters, but with less violence than in explosive eruptions; it may be the initial phase of opening the volcanic conduit (fig. 9).

In phreatomagmatic eruptions, however, there is direct contact between magma and water inside the volcanic conduit during the process of fragmentation, when the mix of gas and magma is subject to an abrupt depression, due to its expansion and acceleration. The instantaneous evaporation of water creates enormous pressure, which in turn accentuates the fragmentation of the magma, creating an increase in the explosiveness and violence of the eruptive event (fig. 10). This kind of eruption is typified by the formation of a cloud of ash, lapilli, and large ring-shaped (base-surge) pyroclasts at the base of the eruptive column. This cloud expands at high velocity and in all directions down the sides of the volcano.

11a. Structure of Somma-Vesuvius, with the Great Cone in the foreground and the crest of Somma in the background.

11b. Excursion to Vesuvius (photo G. Sommer, late 1800s).

11c. The funicular railway at Vesuvius (photo G. Sommer, late 1800s).

CHRONOLOGY OF VESUVIAN ERUPTIONS

In terms of its configuration, Somma-Vesuvius is one of the most typical compound volcanoes, made up of two structures: the Great Cone of Vesuvius (1,280 meters) formed within the caldera of the older structure of Somma (1,132 meters), which appears as a truncated cone with a diameter of approximately 4 kilometers. A

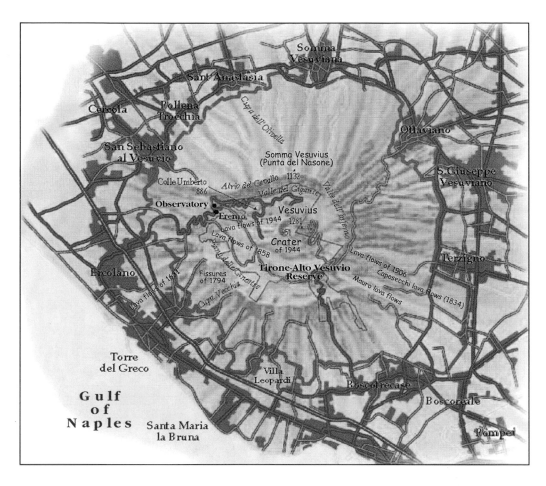

Somma
Vesuviana

Sant'Anastasia

Cercola

Pollena
Trocchia

San Sebastiano
al Vesuvio

Colle Umberto
886

Observatory

Eremo

Ercolano

Cupa dell'Olivella

Atrio del Cavallo 1132

Valle del Gigante

Somma Vesuvius
(Punta del Nasone)

Ottaviano

S. Giuseppe
Vesuviano

Vesuvius
1281

Lava flows of 1944
951

Crater
of 1944

Lava Flows of 1858

Fissures
of 1794

Tirone-Alto Vesuvio
Reserve

Valle dell'Inferno

Lava flows of 1906

Caposecchi lava flows

Mauro lava flows

Mauro lava Flows (1834)

Terzigno

Lava flows of 1631

Cupa Vecchia

Torre
del Greco

Villa
Leopardi

Boscotrecase

Boscoreale

Gulf
of
Naples

Santa Maria
la Bruna

Pompei

large, deep, semicircular valley, 5 kilometers long and 500 meters wide, called the Valley of the Giant, separates the two structures. Its northwestern section is known as the Atrium of the Horse, and it lies northeast of the Valley of the Inferno, with open plains to the south and the Plain of Broom to the west (fig. 12). Morphologically the Somma caldera is made up of a mountainous crest to the north and a depression to the south. The crest, shaped like an amphitheater, is called the Cognoli, and its highest point is the Punta del Nasone (1,130

meters). The depression, the Atrium of the Horse, is shaped like a ring around the cone of Vesuvius, at the center of the caldera. It resulted from the destructive effects of the paroxysmal Plinian eruptions that shook the volcanic structure during the last twenty-five thousand years, repeatedly demolishing the upper portion of the mountain and creating a large depression within which the cone of Vesuvius was formed. The volcanic structure of the Great Cone, visible today, is a stratovolcano, made up of alternating layers of lava and pyroclastic materials, which have

12. Map of the volcanic complex of Somma-Vesuvius, showing the location of the principal sites.

13. The small central cone within Vesuvius in the 1930s.

accumulated over the course of the last 350 years. This was the most recent phase of the volcano's activity (1631–1944), after the disastrous eruption of 1631 had demolished the preexisting structure. This phase was characterized by fewer explosive manifestations of the Strombolian type, with an open conduit. Small cones of scoria (fig. 13) sometimes formed within the Vesuvius crater, which were later destroyed by more violent eruptions. The present-day crater of the Great Cone was formed after the last eruption of 1944; it has a diameter of approximately 500 meters and a depth of approximately 200–250 meters (fig. 14).

Although it is not known with certainty when the volcano first became active, after dating lava and volcanic materials discovered during the sinking of a geothermal well in the area of Trecase, it was estimated that the oldest structure, Somma, was already active three hundred thousand years ago. Its eruptive history can be reconstructed in sufficient detail, beginning twenty-five thousand years ago, the age of a paleo soil discovered beneath a level of pumice that can be ascribed to Somma and localized in a pit near the town of Codola. This ancient layer covers deposits of Campanian ignimbrite (gray tuff or volcanic ash). The ignimbrite is evidence of an extremely violent pyroclastic flow that originated in the Phlegraean area, which approximately thirty-five thousand years ago covered more than 500 square kilometers. The Somma edifice was built through low energy activity, predominantly of the effusive and weakly explosive type. Only activity of this type could create such an impressive volcanic structure, estimated at approximately 3,000 meters tall. Beginning twenty-five thousand years ago Somma began a new type of predominantly explosive activity.

Since that time the behavior of the volcanic complex has been changeable, with at least eight cycles that seem to display the following pattern:

- Plinian eruption
- Inter-Plinian activity
- Period of dormancy

Each of these cycles began with an extremely violent explosive eruption in a closed conduit (Plinian eruption), after a long interval of quiescence (period of dormancy). There followed a period of persistent low-energy activity with minor explosiveness, of a predominantly effusive character with an open conduit (inter-Plinian activity), before a subsequent phase of dormancy. There have been eight major Plinian eruptions, recognizable by the pyroclastic deposits discovered in the areas of Vesuvius. They are as follows: *Codola* (25,000 years ago), *Sarno* (22,000 years ago), *Basal Pumice* (17,000 years ago), *Verdoline [pale green] Pumice* (15,000 years ago), *Lagno Amendolare* (11,400 years ago), *Mercato* (8,000 years ago), *Avellino* (3,600 years ago), and *Pompeii* (A.D. 79) (See table of eruptions, pp. 125–126).
It should be noted that the reconstruction of all the most violent eruptions of Somma-Vesuvius that have occurred in recent centuries has been carried out with the help of studies conducted on lands surrounding the volcano. Through these studies it has been possible to reconstruct a chronological sequence of the major eruptive phases. A significant contribution was made by absolute datings made with the carbon-14 method, on substances of organic origin (paleo soils) that formed in areas exposed to atmospheric alterations during the volcano's periods of dormancy.
Often these eruptions were followed by lava flow activity that disturbed the volcano's supply system in such a way that the magma's rise was facilitated. The violent eruption of A.D. 79 buried the settlements along the volcano's slopes. It was the latest Plinian event to disturb the volcanic edifice after

14. The crater of the Great Cone of Vesuvius as it appears today.

15. The small central cone of Vesuvius, photographed in the autumn of 1934.

approximately 500–700 years of quiescence. The previous eruption of a significant size prior to the one of 79 dates to the beginning of the eighth century B.C. Deposits from this eruption have been identified on the terrain. But probably other not very violent eruptions occurred before the pre-79 phase of dormancy. These left only small deposits, difficult to trace on the terrain after the passage of time. The great explosive events of 472 and 1631, on the other hand, were categorized as sub-Plinian, in that they were less violent than Plinian eruptions and produced a smaller volume of pyroclastic materials. The inter-Plinian activity between the eruptions of Avellino and Pompeii was very intense, followed by a quiet period of about five hundred to seven hundred years before the eruption of A.D. 79.

The inter-Plinian activity between the eruptions of 79 and 472 was less intense, with a quiescence of 170 years. In contrast, the subsequent inter-Plinian activity lasted about 700 years, followed by a period of dormancy of at least 130 years, before the last explosive eruption of 1631. The year 1944 was characterized by a series of eruptive events that were predominantly Strombolian in nature, interspersed with more or less brief periods of quiet. The activity was nearly continuous, with numerous quiet flows localized around the crater or along preferential fault lines. In general three eruptive typologies can be identified for Vesuvius:
A) Eruptions with an open conduit, subdivided into:
- non-paroxysmal eruptions with an open conduit,

characterized by slow, tranquil emissions of magma resulting in the formation of vast lava bodies (Colle Margherita in 1891–1894 and Colle Umberto in 1895–1899);
- paroxysmal eruptions with an open conduit of the Strombolian type, with the extrusion of lava and scoria that led to the formation of small cones within the Great Cone of Vesuvius, where subsequent activity would be concentrated (fig. 15);
- paroxysmal eruptions with an open conduit, characterized by effusive phases, with lava flows that can last considerable lengths of time, and by explosive phases, sometimes extremely violent, in which fountains of lava form and notable quantities of pyroclastic materials (ash, pumice, scoria, etc.) fall; in the end they lead to the destruction of the small inner cone and to the expansion of the crater of the Great Cone (eruption of 1944) (fig. 16);

B) paroxysmal eruptions of average scale with a closed conduit, such as those of A.D. 472 and 1631, categorized as sub-Plinian, with the formation of a sub-caldera (the Vesuvius caldera). These eruptions can cause the destruction of the Great Cone of Vesuvius and are characterized by deposits of fallen pumice, pyroclastic flows, and mud flows (lahars);

C) catastrophic, paroxysmal eruptions with a closed conduit, categorized as

16. The eruption of March 1944 in its terminal phase.

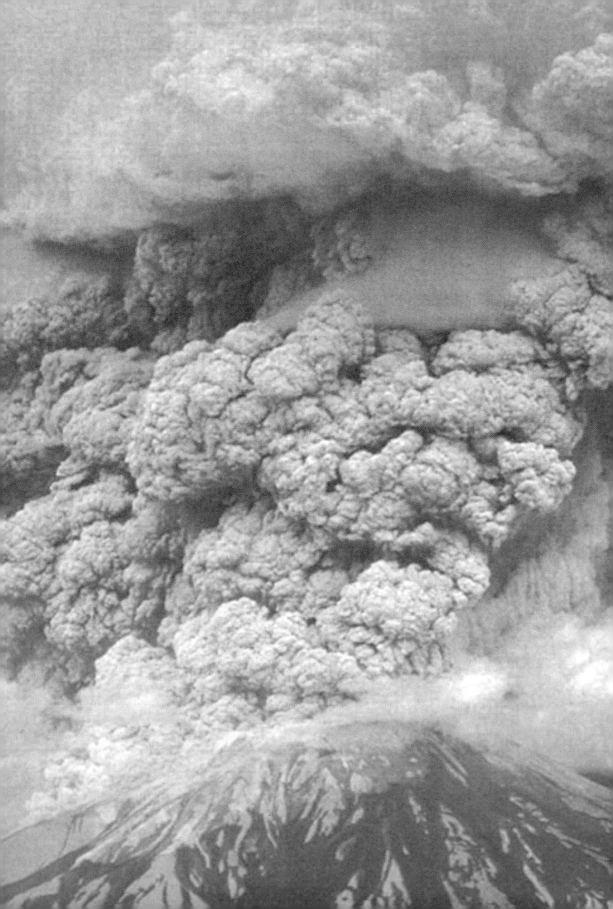

Plinian, like the eruption of A.D. 79, which occur after a long period of inactivity and in the presence of a volcanic conduit obstructed by solidified materials from the last eruption, leading to the formation or expansion of a caldera (the Somma caldera). These are characterized by emissions of pyroclastic materials of considerable quantity, flows, and greater energy compared to sub-Plinian and lahar eruptions (fig. 17).

The volcano's current phase of dormancy has lasted for fifty-eight years, leading to the supposition that Vesuvius may be entering a new period of inactivity, presaging a subsequent reawakening of an explosive nature, probably similar to the eruption of 1631. This supposition is based on the now-confirmed cyclical development of Somma-Vesuvius for more than three thousand years, based on statistical studies.

The Proto-historical Activity of Vesuvius

The Plinian eruptions, which can be verified beginning twenty-five thousand years ago and recognized on the terrain, are the most violent to have shaken the volcanic edifice, depositing great quantities of pyroclastic materials over extensive areas. In contrast, the weakest eruptions, which occurred when there was an open conduit, generally have left few deposits. Traces of these are difficult to find in the surrounding country after the passage of time; they have been removed easily by subsequent activity.

It should be kept in mind that in reality we cannot reconstruct what occurred in the intervals of time between the violent Plinian events: detectable data on the terrain that relate to very precise periods of activity are so scarce that we can only assume that low-energy eruptions of a predominantly effusive nature have taken place. One Plinian event worth noting is the eruption of the so-called Pumice of Avellino (the extruded materials were discovered for the first time in the province of Avellino), which took place approximately 3,600 years ago, around 1600 B.C. This was the last great event of this type that shook the volcanic edifice prior to the eruption of A.D. 79. The deposits from this eruption, which consisted of white and gray pumice and ash layers consistent with surge activity, covered many sites from the Early Bronze Age in the area north-northeast of the volcano. This eruption claimed numerous victims among the resident population, as we know from an extraordinary discovery in San Paolo Belsito, near Nola: two bodies lie stretched out on the layer of white pumice, killed by the gaseous fumes emitted by the pyroclastics (fig. 18). The area more directly affected by this catastrophic event, particularly

18. Female skeleton recently discovered in San Paolo Belsito, on the layer of pumice from the Avellino eruption.

17. Paroxysmal phase of the eruption of Mount St. Helens in May 1980.

19. Burial sites at the necropolis of S. Abbondio (Pompeii).

the sector northeast of the Campanian territory, was reduced to desert over a period of centuries and abandoned by the surviving population, with a consequent disappearance of every form of productive life. In contrast, human habitation continued in the marginal areas: a recent important discovery demonstrates the existence of a settlement with materials that can be dated to the eighteenth century B.C. (Early Bronze Age) and a necropolis that can be dated to the seventeenth–sixteenth centuries B.C. (beginning of the Middle Bronze Age), along the southern ridge of the hill of Sant'Abbondio, approximately 700 meters southeast of the built-up area of Pompeii (fig. 19).

The proximity of the sea, whose coastline was considerably farther inland than it was in later eras, and the mouth of the Sarno River, which ran near the southern ridge of the hill, were decisive factors in the choice of this site for burials, since there is ample archaeological evidence that in the Bronze Age the worship of the dead was closely tied to watercourses.

Subsequently the areas surrounding the volcano were subject to at least three other important eruptive events. The first two occurred 3,200–3,400 years ago, a short time after the catastrophic eruption of Avellino, with consequences that clearly were less dramatic for those who inhabited the affected areas. The third event occurred around the beginning of the eighth century B.C. The dating of the latter event, which has been confirmed by recent radiometric datings and was probably followed by a period of predominantly effusive activity, makes it possible to estimate a period of dormancy lasting at least five hundred years, preceding the eruption of A.D. 79. This interval of time was sufficient for the populations that returned to inhabit the mountain's slopes to lose any historical memory of the nearby mountain's danger.

Activity between 79 and 1631

In the years following the eruption of A.D. 79, the entire area was covered with volcanic material, turning it into desert for all practical purposes. Consequently all productive life disappeared and the population that had escaped the disaster migrated, probably in the direction of Naples and Nuceria. The entire road network also vanished, including the important axis that, reaching the two urban centers of Pompeii and Herculaneum, linked Nuceria to Naples and to the maritime port of Pozzuoli [Latin name Puteoli]. This loss was significant for the economy of the entire region.

Sources in our possession related to the period after A.D. 79 are very scarce and focus essentially either on the desolate appearance of the area around Vesuvius after the eruption, or on the divine wrath that had punished Pompeii and Herculaneum. However some authors, including Statius in A.D. 94, have left important accounts about the new habitation of the territory: *Do not believe that the summit of Vesuvius and the fiery waves that flowed down the maleficent mountain have totally depopulated the anxious cities: inhabitants are there, indeed they prosper and grow in number* (*Silvae* III, 5, 72–75); *or the salutary pools of Ischia or Stabiae that have been reborn* (*Silvae* III, 5, 104).

This important passage by Statius and numerous archaeological discoveries show a new post-79 settlement of the area, which must have occurred as soon as the early second century A.D., with the rebuilding of the principal roadways as well. However, we have no evidence regarding the rebuilding of extensive urban centers or a new system of residential villas in the coastal area that characterized this section of Campania prior to A.D. 79. The entire area probably would have had a network of small farms devoted to agriculture and livestock, with economic activities that were broadly connected but not capable of bringing the economy of the Vesuvian territory up to the level of wealth and the variety of production that had characterized the previous period. After A.D. 79 the activity of Vesuvius was characterized by phases with an open conduit, with magmatic extrusions for periods that lasted as long as scores of years, alternating with periods of calm for some centuries before the sub-Plinian eruptions of 472 and 1631. It is noteworthy that the persistence of volcanic phenomena, which culminated in the eruptions of 203 and 472, continued to hinder the area's development and any possible rebirth of its urban centers. (CASSIUS DIO, *Historia Romana*, LXXVI, 2, 1: *In that time Vesuvius spewed forth an immense quantity of fire and the force of this explosion was so great that it was felt as far as Capua, where I reside when I stay in Italy.*) The eruption of A.D. 472 was characterized by the deposit of greenish pumice and large quantities of material from surges and pyroclastic flows in the northeast sector of the volcano. Other eruptions of a significant magnitude, which we know about from contemporary accounts, date

20. The Somma-Vesuvius structure before the eruption of 1631 (N. Perrey, seventeenth century, engraving).

back to 512 (this event was sufficiently violent for Theodoric, king of the Goths, to exempt the survivors from paying taxes), 685, 787, 968, 999, 1007, 1037, and 1139. Subsequently there is information about light Strombolian and fumarolic activity, at least until the early years of the fourteenth century. There is debate, however about the testimony of Ambrogio Leone da Nola, with regard to an eruption that occurred around 1500:
For three days we saw extremely dark air… when the eruptive violence, which in spewing volcanic material, had covered everything in sight, reddish ash rained down in great abundance…
(*De Nola opusculum, 1514*).
This reference, which is not mentioned by any other author, raises doubts about whether the eruption actually occurred. Probably there were weak phreatic explosions, caused by rising magma heating the waters of an acquifer, with weak emissions of ash. Finally, in the early 1600s there are

accounts telling of pools of rainwater at the bottom of the crater, heated by hot vapor rich in acidic substances, probably related to the rising of magmatic fluids toward the surface (fig. 20).

The Eruption of 1631

The eruption of December 1631, the most catastrophic for this volcano in modern times, was an event of fundamental importance in the history of Vesuvius. Not only did this mark the beginning of the most recent cycle of activity after a repose of at least 130 years but also, thanks to the numerous historical documents from subsequent decades and centuries, this event made it possible to obtain useful information and descriptions about the volcano's activity. These have allowed us to study its dynamics.
As early as July, the population of the area had noted earthquakes that intensified in the days before the eruption. *The Torresi* [inhabitants of Torre

del Greco] *and of course the inhabitants of Massa di Somma, Polena, and San Bastiano, recalled that since December 10 they had been hearing rumbling in the mountain, with so much moving about of subterranean spirits that they could not sleep well at night….* (GIULIO CESARE BRACCINI, *Dell'incendio fattosi sul Vesuvio a XVI di dicembre MDCXXXI…*, Naples, 1632)

In late November some shepherds going to the summit of Vesuvius noted that the bottom of the crater had risen so much that it almost reached the edge, probably a sign that the earth was swelling within the cone due to the pressure of the magma. A couple of days before the eruption, according to the testimony of some shepherds who climbed to the volcano's summit, it was confirmed that the surface shook continuously and in some wells the water level had risen, while in others there was no water or it was muddy. Probably these phenomena indicated a rising of the earth due to the increase of magmatic pressure, but no one thought it indicated an imminent resumption of the volcano's activity.

On the night of December 15, the earthquakes became progressively more numerous and were noticed by the populations around the volcano. The intensification of these events in the hours immediately preceding the eruption probably was linked to the fracturing of the Great Cone. Toward midnight, flashes were noted at the summit of the crater, both from Ponte della Maddalena and near Naples, as well as from Resina, present-day Herculaneum. This was the opening phase of the volcanic conduit, which was characterized by Strombolian activity with the first emissions of pyroclastic material.

Around 6:30 a.m. on December 16, another violent earthquake was felt, followed by a seismic swarm toward 7:00 a.m. Meanwhile a fracture opened up on the western side of the Great Cone, extending from the summit of Vesuvius down to the base of the Somma caldera plane, from which gas and ash violently spewed forth, along with the first showers of incandescent blocks and scoria. In the hours that followed, people witnessed the formation of a Plinian umbrella-shaped column that rose about 40 kilometers. At the same time the first ash began to flow. The ash made up the densest part of the cloud that, collapsing beneath its own weight, slid down the sides of the volcano. Between 8:00 and 10:00 a.m. there was a dense rain of ash, followed by an extrusion of blocks and scoria, which fell in the area east of the volcano until 6:00 p.m. Around 1:00 p.m. the vapors and gases emitted from the chasm grew so thick that it became dark and difficult to breathe in Naples, toward which part of the column was impelled. This was the most violent phase of the eruption, characterized by a well-developed column. It was accompanied by a continuous seismic tremor felt in the city of Naples beginning at 10:00 in the morning, and lasting for approximately another ten hours. Meanwhile in the afternoon the stratospheric winds blowing toward the east transported the lighter materials to Publia and as far as the

21. The 1631 eruption of Vesuvius, with the procession of the relics of San Gennaro (Micco Spadaro, 1609–1675, oil on canvas).

Yugoslavian coasts. At the same time the Viceroy of Naples, the Count of Monterrey, organized a procession that carried the blood and head of San Gennaro through the streets, in the vain hope of mitigating the effects of the eruption. In the downwind areas and those closer to the volcano, pumice, ash, bombs, and other materials from the crater continued to fall. Towards evening there was a succession of jolts that became more frequent during the night. During the night of December 16 to 17, around 2:00 in the morning, a cloud of incandescent material was expelled from the summit of the crater; it fell below into the valley between the cone of Vesuvius and Somma. Moreover, intense rain, mobilizing the ash deposited on the slopes of the volcano, created lahar (mud flows) on the north sides of Somma,

which caused tremendous damage.

At 8:00 on the morning of December 17 another column of material caused a downpour of lapilli, incandescent blocks, and ash, southeast of the volcano. Towards midday a violent earthquake was felt in Naples, probably linked to a collapse that occurred in the depths of the volcano, which would have led to the collapse of the crater. Meanwhile, the volcano emitted an enormous mass of pyroclasts, ash, and gas, which poured down the sides of the volcano and destroyed the surrounding areas. The emission of red-hot clouds was accompanied by the withdrawal of the sea along the entire coast of the Gulf of Naples for approximately ten minutes, which probably was connected to a swelling of the soil caused by enormous pressure within the magmatic chamber. The heavy rains of the morning caused the formation of further avalanches of mud, which continued until 2:00 in the afternoon, overwhelming everything that came in their path.

In the afternoon Cardinal Buoncompagno organized a second procession with the relics of San Gennaro:

In bringing the Holy Relic out of the Cathedral portal the rain ceased completely and the sun suddenly appeared…. But thereafter it is understood that from the large portal window of the Cathedral… there appeared clearly to the people gathered in the piazza the glorious Saint Gennaro himself, in his pontifical habit, who blessed the people from the window and then disappeared (GIOVAN BATTISTA MANSO, *Lettere da Napoli*, 1631) (fig. 21).

The procession crossed Porta Capuana, carrying on to a knoll from which Vesuvius was visible, and as soon as the Cardinal exposed the relics in the direction of the volcano:

lo and behold the immeasurable, high, and intemperate cloud fell from the summit, almost bowing its head to the holy relic…. All the people cried out….aloud at the new miracle…. so that in a moment the entire immeasurable cloud dispersed, so that the mountain appeared, which until then had not been seen (fig. 22).

In effect, oddly enough, it was precisely in the afternoon that the fall of ash upon the city lessened, due to a change in wind direction, and the eruptive activity began to subside, with moderate emissions of ash and isolated explosions that diminished in intensity in the days that followed. Meanwhile seismic activity was noted for several more months. The violence of the eruption had destroyed the

22. The Somma-Vesuvius structure after the eruption of 1631, with the representation of San Gennaro (N. Perrey, seventeenth century, engraving).

23. Tourists visiting the small central cone of Vesuvius, after the eruption of 1933.

24a. Eruption of Vesuvius in the eighteenth century, observed from the Ponte della Maddalena, near Naples (Anonymous, eighteenth century, engraving with watercolor).

earlier Vesuvian cone, reducing the height of the edifice by about 470 meters, with the formation of a caldera 1.5 kilometers in diameter, the edges of which were extremely unstable. Finally, at the bottom of the crater, scores of openings were visible, each of which emitted a plume of white smoke, while at the sides of the volcano towards Torre del Greco, lateral openings appeared. The eruption claimed about ten thousand victims from the local population and also caused extremely severe damage to the buildings and to economic activities.

As a warning to future populations, in 1632 the Viceroy had a memorial tablet, still visible today, brought to Granatello di Portici, as a reminder of the terrible eruption. The text on the tablet exhorts future generations to flee immediately at the first signs of Vesuvius's reawakening, before the fury of the volcano can strike.

24a

Vesuvian Activity between 1631 and 1944

Following the eruption of 1631, predominantly Strombolian activity was established in the Vesuvius caldera. This period was characterized by explosions and frequent fountains of lava, which contributed to the construction of a new Great Cone. From 1631 until 1944 there were some eighteen periods of small- and medium-intensity activity, with localized eruptions at both the central opening and side openings. Each eruptive period, preceded by an interval of quiet lasting at most seven years and characterized only by fumarolic activity, began with a gradual increase in the intensity of the explosive phenomena (Strombolian in nature), with the emission of lava and scoria from fractures that originated at the crater floor. This continuous activity, which could last for months, contributed to the building of a small cone of scoria within the Great Cone, where eruptive phenomena were later concentrated. Meanwhile the continuous lava flows helped to fill the crater, the bottom of which rose up to the brim (fig. 23). The final phase of each eruptive period was distinguished by a violent paroxysm that led to the destruction of the small inner cone and to the amplification of the crater. The end of each active period was followed by a new period of quiescence. Some of the most significant eruptive events to take place during this phase of Vesuvius's activity were those of 1660, 1694, 1698, 1707, 1737 (the first that occurred with the Great Cone rebuilt as far as the height of Somma), 1760, 1767, 1779, 1794, 1822 (the most violent of the nineteenth century, causing the Great Cone to drop about 100 meters), 1834, 1850, 1855, 1861, 1872, 1906 (the largest eruption of the last century, in which the Great Cone dropped 300 meters), and 1929 (figs. 24 a–b–c, 25–26). In particular, during the second half of the eighteenth century, between 1767 and 1794, a series of violent eruptions destroyed numerous villages, claiming many victims among the farmers who lived along the slopes of the mountain. Sir William Hamilton, the famous English ambassador to the court of Ferdinand IV of Bourbon, who is considered a forerunner of present-day volcanologists, was an observant collector and scholar of antiquity. He was disconcerted by the stubborn fatalism of the farmers and inhabitants of the villages, who did not even consider abandoning their houses, even though Vesuvius continued to threaten the territory:

The phenomena of nature are slow. Each farmer lives in the pitiful illusion that an eruption will never take place during his lifetime, or, should it occur, he hopes that his protector saint will keep the destructive lava away from his field; and in truth the great fertility of the soil in the vicinity of the volcano draws people to live in these places. (W. HAMILTON, *The Phlegraean Fields*, Naples, 1779).

The saint that Hamilton mentions was San Gennaro, patron of Naples. When Vesuvius resumed its activity, the saint's statue was carried in procession through the streets, that the city might obtain his protection. It is due to this tradition that scholars have found evidence regarding the eruptions of Vesuvius in the parish records, where the dates of the processions were inscribed

24b. Eruption of Vesuvius from Mergellina (P. Fabris, 1779, etching with watercolor).

24b

(fig. 27). Today one still can see the statue of San Gennaro on the Ponte della Maddalena, east of the city, commemorating the eruption of 1767. The saint is depicted with his open hand outstretched toward the volcano, in the act of stopping the flow of lava. Another statue can be found in Ottaviano, where the saint is depicted with vials of blood in his hand, referring to his famous miracle and in remembrance of the eruption of 1737. And in Naples a bust of the saint sits in a niche near the Porta Capuana, in front of the Church of Santa Caterina a Formiello, in remembrance of the eruption of 1707.

Regarding the impact of the winds on the distribution of the materials produced by explosive eruptions in

24c. Eruption of Vesuvius from Mergellina (P. Fabris, 1779, etching with watercolor).

25. The eruption of Vesuvius of 1872 (photo G. Sommer).

27. San Gennaro in Glory with Vesuvius and the city of Naples in the background (J. De Ribera, 1591–1652, oil on canvas).

26. The eruption of Vesuvius of 1906, with a group of people fleeing from the surrounding areas.

28. The eruption of Vesuvius of 1944, observed from Capodichino (Naples).

the area surrounding Vesuvius, Braccini described the catastrophe of 1831 and mentioned the Saint's intervention:

Why has the ash that spewed from the cavity of Vesuvius always moved more to the east and south than to the west and north? It makes sense to me to believe that this has occurred through the continuing miracle and through the special grace granted by God to the city of Naples, for one thousand two hundred years, through the intercession of the glorious martyr San Gennaro....

The Eruption of 1944

The last eruption of the volcano occurred in the midst of a war and represented the concluding event of the cycle of activity that had begun in 1631. Giuseppe Imbò, the director of the Vesuviuan Observatory at the time, followed this eruption through all its phases with scientific scrupulousness and dedication, and under conditions of great precariousness. In December of 1943 the American forces put seismographic equipment at his disposal, to follow the activity of Vesuvius. The eruption began on the afternoon of March 18, when the volcanic conduit abruptly reopened, resulting in intense effusive and explosive activity. The first lava flows began to fill the chasm that formed after the collapse of the small cone inside the crater. This then overflowed and created two flows, the first of which moved northward, reaching the wall of Somma in about an hour, while the second poured down partly along the outside of the cone, pushing downhill, and partly along the southwest walls of the crater. Meanwhile the explosive activity became more intense with a shower of pyroclasts expelled to a height of approximately 100 meters, and at a distance from the mouth of no more than 100 meters. The activity was more or less constant until the morning of the 19th, when, in consequence of new magma flows, streams of lava poured outside the crater, while the expulsion of pyroclastic materials intensified. A new flow began during the night and was distributed along the north slope. It poured into the earlier flows, moving rapidly downhill to reach the towns of Massa and San Sebastiano al Vesuvio on the morning of the 20th (fig. 28). A new eruptive phase began in the afternoon and was characterized by violent lava fountains, each lasting about one hour and reaching heights of between 500 and 1,000 meters, interspersed with brief pauses. At the same time, lava flows on both slopes diminished. This phase lasted until the morning of the 22nd. It was followed immediately by violent emissions of ash and incandescent scoria from an eruptive cloud with the characteristic volcanic umbrella formation, which reached a height of approximately 3,000 meters. At intervals, partial collapses of the cloud created small, red-hot flows (fig. 29). The effusive activity now came to an end, while the explosive activity, somewhat reduced in intensity, continued in the same manner as in the preceding days. Then a series of violent earthquakes began. On the morning of March 24, Vesuvius looked as if it were blanketed in snow

29. March 24, 1944; the eruption observed from Pompeii, with the campanile of the Marian Sanctuary in the foreground. One can see the lightning flashes caused by the friction of particles emitted into the atmosphere.

due to the copious quantity of light colored ash, representing the terminal phase of the event. In the days that followed there was a gradual sinking of the lava shelf that created a chasm about 200–300 meters deep (fig. 30).

The activity continued with lesser intensity until early April, emitting only clouds of very fine ash. Then the eruptive mouth, which had already been obstructed in a continuous series of landslides and reopenings, closed completely. From that point on Vesuvius entered a phase of dormancy, losing the characteristic wreath of smoke that, since the eruption of 1631, had been a distinctive feature of the Neapolitan landscape, indicating which way the winds were blowing (fig. 31). This quiescence was interrupted only by episodic seismic crises, the last of which occurred in October of 1999, and by normal weak fumarolic manifestations, the sole evidence of the volcano's continuing vitality.

Phenomena Forewarning Eruptions

Warning phenomena are tied to the rising of the magma toward the earth's surface. This rise provokes an upward shift of hot masses, whose movements can be detected through sophisticated monitoring equipment. Generally in volcanic areas the resumption of eruptive activity may be preceded by the following premonitory phenomena: The warping of rocks, seen on the surface as gradual swellings of the volcanic area; fracturing of

rocks, which creates tell-tale vibrations that indicate an increase of shallow seismic activity near the volcano; and an increase in the surface temperature of the fumaroles, with expulsions of volcanic gases that escape from the magma and heat the circulating surface water, which in turn supplies the fumaroles. In any case it should be kept in mind that the precursor phenomena are connected to an eruptive process that is already underway. Its evolution over a certain period of time depends substantially on the velocity of the phenomena, which are difficult to assess. The main problem with prediction lies in understanding the particular eruptive type of a volcano. It is very difficult to identify the precise succession of events that will take place before an eruption. In fact, the same phenomena occur at different preceding stages, depending on the characteristics of the volcano and the magma that feeds its activity.

For this reason it is of fundamental importance to construct a physical model of the volcano, on the basis of empirical data that allow scientists to generate predictions about its eruptive activity. However it is possible that pre-eruptive phenomena might run a different course from those determined empirically, since a volcano can change its type of activity, above all if it has been quiescent for a long time. This situation poses hard questions about the dynamics that will distinguish its reawakening. There is no doubt that the verification of premonitory phenomena indicates an

30. The eruption of 1944, seen from Sorrento, with the eruptive column that rose more than 4 kilometers in height.

31. View of Vesuvius from Naples in the early years of the twentieth century, before the eruption of 1906, with the characteristic plume of smoke.

anomalous state for a volcano that may have an eruptive episode. But the prediction of this episode is made more difficult by the fact that eruptions do not always follow premonitory signals, as for example in the two crises that occurred in Campania in the area of the Phlegraean Fields in 1970 and 1982, as well as in the caldera of Rabaul (Papua New Guinea) in 1984.

Moreover it has been noted that eruptions of an explosive nature that occur after long periods of dormancy are generally preceded by warnings that are much more obvious and play out over a much broader time frame, compared to quiet-flow eruptions. This difference can be attributed to the great resistance presented by the consolidated rocks of an inactive volcano when magma intrudes from a depth and is more viscous compared to the thinner magma emitted during fluid eruptions.

In the case of Vesuvius, due to historical sources, we know that before the eruption of A.D. 79, seismic activity intensified in the months and days immediately preceding the event. But for the eruption of 1631 the warning signals clearly began at least ten days before the volcano's reawakening. Evidently those who were writing at the time had not even the slightest awareness of the origins of these manifestations. Yet they passed on extremely important information about them, which has made it possible to delineate a general picture of what might happen one day with the resumption of volcanic activity.

It is plausible to believe that the eruption of 1944 might have represented the closure of an eruptive cycle that began in 1631, hypothetically implying a resumption of explosive activity. In fact the maximum event anticipated in the area of Vesuvius, and on the basis of which an evacuation plan has been drawn up, would be an eruption similar to that of 1631.

The volcano's activity is now continuously monitored by the Vesuvius Observatory's thorough surveillance network. The notable stability of Vesuvius today makes it difficult to predict when the volcano might resume its activity. For reasons discussed earlier, Vesuvius will not wake suddenly or without clear warning, as much of the population along the volcano's slopes seems to fear.

Backdrop for the Eruption

LITERARY, ICONOGRAPHIC, AND VOLCANOLOGICAL SOURCES ON THE MORPHOLOGY OF SOMMA-VESUVIUS IN THE FIRST CENTURY A.D.

Vesuvius Mons (the term the ancients used for the current volcanic edifice of Somma-Vesuvius) dominated the entire area. Its appearance prior to the eruption was the subject of numerous studies and heated debates, judging from the various interpretations of literary, archaeological, and volcanological data in our possession (fig. 32). Before entering into the fray, we need to ask if, in Roman times, people knew about the volcanic nature of Vesuvius. Thanks to valuable testimony about the appearance of the area, found in the writings of Strabo, Vitruvius, and Diodorus Siculus, who lived prior to the A.D. 79 eruption, we can resolve this initial problem with some certainty. A passage written by the Greek geographer Strabo is fundamental (*Geography* V, 48, C 246–247) and identified the true nature of the mountain from the burned appearance of its rocks. Strabo surmised that in the past, like Etna, which was then active and whose volcanic origins and fertile terrain were known, Vesuvius might have erupted. Moreover Vitruvius

(*De Architectura* II, 6, 2) stated: *It is said, moreover, that fires burned beneath Vesuvius in the past, and seething, they poured over, flooding the neighboring countryside. Thus it seems that what now is known as sponge-stone, or Pompeian pumice, was another sort of stone, which then was transformed by the fire so that it has this quality.* The brief and incisive testimony of Diodorus Siculus (*Bibliotheca Historica [Historical Library]* IV, 21, 5) finally confirms that the resemblance between Vesuvius and Etna was understood, even in early times. Thus it is evident that the volcanic origins of Vesuvius were well known in Roman times, although curiously Pliny the Elder makes no mention of this in his writings. The long period of

32. Pompeii, Vesuvius, and the surrounding territory, in the first half of the 1800s (A. Guesdon, c. 1855, lithograph).

33. Bacchus and Vesuvius, fresco discovered in Pompeii, in the House of the Centenary.

inactivity evidently had quelled any fears about the mountain's danger for many who lived in its immediate vicinity.

However it is much more difficult to attempt to reconstruct the appearance of Somma-Vesuvius prior to the A.D. 79 eruption. This issue has divided scholars between those who support the hypothesis that a single-peaked volcano existed at the time of the Pompeii eruption, and those who believe it was double-peaked, with the Great Cone of Vesuvius already in place. In the twentieth century, hypothesizing that Vesuvius, an element so characteristic of this entire part of Campania, might have influenced local painting ateliers, wall decorations discovered in residences were examined, in search of definitive proof for one side of the argument or the other. Certain small paintings of mythological subjects and landscapes were scrutinized, in which the mountain in the background of the scene was identified as Vesuvius. But these are secondary elements, generic for this type of small painting, as are trees, rocks, and small sacred or private buildings, used to set the principal scene. And they also are found earlier, in original Hellenistic cartoons, or are sometimes inserted autonomously by local painters in order to embellish a composition. Thus we cannot consider them particularly significant for identifying the appearance of the volcano before A.D. 79. Moreover some of these compositions have been lost and are now known only through nineteenth-century engravings, preventing any possibility of verifying the original painting. But the famous lararium fresco, known as "Bacchus and Vesuvius," now in the National Archaeological Museum in Naples (MANN Inv. No. 112282), is another case entirely. It was discovered in the excavations carried out between 1879 and 1881 in the House of the Centenary in Pompeii, in a connecting space of the house's service area (fig. 33). The central portion of the composition depicts a tall, peaked mountain, its slopes covered by lush vineyards. To the side, almost as if to celebrate the vocation connected to his person, is an unusual and original image of Dionysus with his body in the form of a cluster of grapes. Such a curious painting, unique within the usual panorama provided by lararium frescoes discovered in the area of Vesuvius, led scholars to identify

the single-peaked mountain with the volcano before the eruption. They also found support in numerous ancient literary texts that described the slopes of Vesuvius as covered with extensive vineyards. But even if there is this unquestionable tie between Vesuvius and the grapevine, as sources indicate, we still cannot be sure of its appearance, since the principal text that has been preserved, written by the Greek geographer Strabo (*Geography* V, 4, 8, C 246–247), clearly describes the mountain's shape prior to the eruption:

Mount Vesuvius looms over these centers, covered entirely, except for the peak, with extensive cultivated fields. The summit is for the most part flat, but completely sterile; it is ash-colored in appearance, and has deep depressions like crevices, the reddish rocks of which seem to have been corroded by fire (fig. 34).

The harsh landscape of Vesuvius described in Strabo's passage is also confirmed by Frontinus (c. A.D. 30–103) and by Florus (first–second century A.D.), who relate an episode of the famous rebellion led by the gladiator Spartacus against Rome:

Spartacus himself, weaving ropes with the branches of woodland vines, descended from the summit

34. Reconstruction of Somma-Vesuvius, before the A.D. 79 eruption (Anonymous, second half of the nineteenth century, engraving).

of Vesuvius along that part of the mountain that is apparently inaccessible and therefore unguarded… (*Strategemata* I, 5, 21); [*Spartacus and his hordes, fleeing from Capua toward the south] chose Mount Vesuvius as their first location, almost as if it were the altar of Venus. Here since they were surrounded by Clodius Glabrus, sliding down with cords of vines along the gorges of the mountain's crevices, they descended through a hidden passage to the base and, with a sudden attack, conquered the encampments of the commander who was not expecting anything of the sort…* (*Titus Livy's History II,* 8, 4–5).

Finally we must add to this list of sources a passage by Cassius Dio, who lived between approximately A.D. 155 and 235, and who is known thanks to the Epitome of the monk Xiphilinus, which can be dated to the eleventh century. It is possible that his description refers to the appearance of Vesuvius following the eruption of A.D. 79.

Mount Vesuvius overlooks the sea near Naples and contains extremely copious springs of fire; and at other times its summit had this on all sides, so that fire was found at the center… so the exterior parts never embraced the fire, and only those that were in the middle were consumed by the fire and reduced to ash, the peaks that are around still preserve their height of old; but consumed with the passage of time, the deposits have made the inflamed portion concave; so the entire mountain…has the form of an amphitheater. The elevated parts of this mountain are clad in many trees and vines… (*Hist. Rom.* LXVI, 21-23).

Through literary texts we thus can imagine a single-peaked volcano, with slopes where inaccessible areas alternated with others, more intensely cultivated, especially with vineyards, while the summit, with very scant vegetation, must have been flattened and concave within.

Thus on the basis of information provided by these passages, it becomes clear that a direct connection between the fresco of the House of the Centenary and the appearance of the volcano is not certain.

It is very likely that the unknown Pompeian painter, depicting Dionysus close to a tall mountain, had wanted to portray Vesuvius ideally. Thus it was shown from a distance, with its mass standing out above the surrounding territory, and its slopes cultivated with vineyards, without any pretext of providing a "photographic" image. Finally a new comparison with another fresco has recently been suggested. This artwork was discovered in the excavations carried out between 1853 and 1868, which brought to light the House of the Citharist. The painting (MANN, Inv. No. 112282) depicts an amorous encounter between two figures identified as Venus and Mars or Dido and Aeneas. Behind the figures is a tall mountain with steep slopes and a broad, flat summit, which has been identified with the appearance of the volcano before the eruption (fig. 35).

While this hypothesis is quite engaging, it is still difficult to accept comparisons of this type, as we have already noted with regard to other Pompeian paintings. It is impossibile to demonstrate with certainty the

35. Mars and Venus, fresco discovered in Pompeii in the House of the Citharist (N. La Volpe, c. 1838–1870, drawing).

36. The present-day Great Cone of Vesuvius.

relationship between a generic secondary element in a painting and a real image of the volcano. Therefore beyond the iconographic and literary sources we can only rely on the in-depth studies of volcanology, which have intensified in recent decades, in attempting to reconstruct the image of Somma-Vesuvius prior to the A.D. 79 eruption. In this regard, certain things must be taken into consideration. First of all, an eruption of a Plinian type such as the one in A.D. 79 would have a strong destructive effect on the pre-existing volcanic structures (the inner Great Cone), creating a caldera. Secondly, the Great Cone also could be demolished during sub-Plinian events, as with the eruption of 1631, and rebuilt in less than a century, thanks to subsequent inter-Plinian activity.

In conclusion, even if a conical structure had developed within the Somma caldera after the catastrophic eruption of Avellino, it would have been destroyed by a subsequent sub-Plinian event. So prior to A.D. 79, in keeping with descriptions handed down by ancient sources and consistent with the morphological evolution of the volcano, the edifice appeared truncated at the top and concave within, curiously similar to a large amphitheater without an inner cone. This is how it appears, with the benefit of the doubt, in the aforementioned fresco from the House of the Citharist in Pompeii. A possible new cone, formed through inter-Plinian activity following the eruption of A.D. 79, was demolished by the event of 472. The Great Cone, therefore, was certainly present before the eruption of 1631 and was depicted in images from that time. It developed during inter-Plinian activity in the Middle Ages, in association above all with the significant lava flows of the tenth and eleventh centuries, then to be destroyed in turn by the eruption of 1631 (fig. 36).

THE SARNO RIVER

Another important component in the eruption scenario is the Sarno river, which ran in the immediate vicinity of Pompeii and has been used as an active, navigable waterway since ancient times, thanks to the capacity and regularity of its flow. It linked the port of Pompeii with the nearby centers of Nuceria and Acerrae (STRABO, *Geography* V, 4, 8, C 246–257).

Thanks to the reliable navigability of much of its course, the use of its waters for irrigating the surrounding lands, made fertile by the volcanic material emitted long before by Vesuvius, and the vast marshy areas at the level of its mouth, the Sarno was extremely important for the economic life of this part of Campania. Indeed it was personified and honored almost as a divinity. Vesuvian wall paintings contain depictions in which the Sarno assumes the usual aspect of a river god. It appears as a male figure, stretched out, with a flowing beard and typical attributes such as marsh reeds and a vase from which water flows forth. One such portrayal is in the famous painting from the House of the Sarno Lararium in Pompeii (figs. 37–38) and in another painting, recently discovered in Murecine, in the immediate vicinity of the river mouth. The latter painting shows a personification of the Sarno with a lively scene related to the transport of goods along the watercourse: a boat with two oarsmen, laden with products that have already been weighed on a scale, and two donkeys on shore that help the boat along, towing it with ropes.

The Sarno originates from a series of springs that constitute a major water supply. These are located on the slopes of the massif of Mount Saro, behind the present-day town of the same name, on the slopes of Pizzo d'Alvano. The mountain has a basin that covers an area of approximately 380 square kilometers, including, in addition to the territory of the plain, a secondary artery comprising the riverbeds of the Solofrana and the Cavaiola. After a course of 24 kilometers, and after moving beyond the city of Pompeii to the south, the river empties into the sea near the cliffs of Rovigliano.

The plain into which the Sarno flows represents the southern portion of the much more extensive Campanian plain. It is bound on the east by the calcareous heights of the Lattari Mountains, on the west by the Picentine Mountains, on the northwest by the volcanic structure of Somma-Vesuvius,

37. Pompeii, House of the Sarno Lararium. The Lararium still appears partially covered by pumice (excavations of Amedeo Maiuri in *Regio* I in the 1950s).

and on the southeast by the stretch of coastline between the built-up areas of Torre Annunziata and Castellammare di Stabia. The plain moreover extends for about 200 square kilometers and has been known since antiquity for its flourishing agricultural activity, due to the fertility of the volcanic soil, the favorable climate, and the ample water supply from both the water table and the rivers. The latter are vitally important for this area within the confines of the riverbed. It began once again to empty into the sea, still near the cliffs at Rovigliano, but at a point approximately one kilometer further out than the coastline of A.D. 79.

On the basis of geological tests carried out in recent years, it has been possible to hypothesize a plausible path for the watercourse prior to the eruption. At least in its final stretch at the level of Pompeii, it must have had a rather linear path. After moving alongside the slopes of a modest hilly rise,

38. Pompeii, House of the Sarno Lararium. Detail of the fresco of the Lararium, depicting the personification of the Sarno River and scenes of commercial transport along the waterway.

Sarno hydrographic basin. The catastrophic eruption of A.D. 79, which deposited immense quantities of pyroclastic material over the entire territory, disturbed the geographic profile of the area. It also modified the original course of the river, which probably was shifted slightly north of the current bed, and inevitably interrupted its navigability.

During the years that followed the Sarno must have rebuilt its now known as S. Abbondio, the Sarno built its mouth near the *Petra Herculis* (rocks of Rovigliano), almost where it is today. Recent geo-morphological and paleogeographic studies have shown that near its mouth, the river expanded, creating a marshy area, in part because of the strong presence of surface acquifers. In the parts of this area closer to the coastline, fresh water mixed with seawater, depending on the tides.

The great abundance of both surface water and ground water from the Sarno plains characterized this southern section of the Pompeian territory, but it also must have favored the cultivation of vegetables and fruit, which required continuous irrigation in order to yield optimum harvests. This might help clarify a well-known passage by Columella (*De re rustica* X, 130-136) that mentions *the delightful marshland of Pompeii near the salt works of Hercules*, in a list of sites where cabbages were grown. As Pliny the Elder also noted, this local vegetable was renowned for its tenderness (*Nat. Hist.* XIX, 140).

The term "*dulcis palus*" (delightful marshland) in fact could refer more broadly to the entire area between the coastline, the path of the Sarno River, and the south side of Pompeii, where the abundance of water favored intensive cultivation. The areas closer to the mouth of the river must have been a more truly marshy area, rich in cane thickets and animal life and bordered in turn by narrow strips of woodland. In any case the current state of research does not allow us to more fully define the extent of these areas or their precise location in the territory in question.

Finally, regarding the final stretch of the Sarno's path, there has been much debate and uncertainty as to the existence of a channel connecting the river and the city near the Suburban Baths of the Marine Gate, which would have facilitated the transport of goods by boat. Nor is there a definitive opinion about whether there was a modest tributary, whose source was perhaps along the slopes of Vesuvius, which ran alongside the populated area of Pompeii to the east.

THE COASTLINE IN THE FIRST CENTURY A.D.

The reconstruction of the coastline in the area most directly affected by the eruption of A.D. 79 is a subject that is still under discussion. Its path most probably ran parallel to the current coastline and drawn back on average about one kilometer. Here it skimmed the edge of the built area of Herculaneum, which was constructed on a promontory directly overlooking the sea, and neared the base of the hill of Varano, in the area of Stabiae.

At the farthest areas on the coast affected by the eruption, we have some clear evidence for determining the coastline's position. The precise definition of the central section is more complex, particularly near Pompeii. This part of the territory, including the mouth of the Sarno River and the neighboring marshy area, has always interested scholars, starting with the important work of Michele Ruggiero in the late 1800s, because of its strong connection with the economic life of Pompeii. The salt works of Hercules were located here, as well as the river's port facilities, both maritime and river related. A significant description of this area is found

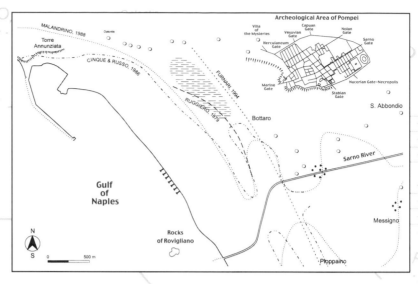

39. Representation of the different reconstructions of the coastline in A.D. 79:

○ Archaeological discoveries;

∴ Cypresses and poplars with roots in soil from A.D. 79 (from Pescatore and others, 1999).

40. Pompeii, area of Bottaro. Excavation of the trench prepared by Francesco Fienga in the 1930s, in order to identify the ancient coastline.

in a passage by Seneca:
Pompeii, celebrated city of Campania, toward which the Sorrentine and Stabian coast converged from one direction, and the Herculanean from the other, closing off the sea, penetrating the mainland, with a magnificent gulf (*Nat. Quaest.* VI, 1, 1–2).
Thus it would seem that the coastline in the vicinity of Pompeii, though straight today, was then undulating, forming a navigable bay or lagoon.
Only recently, on the basis of a series of geological tests conducted both in proximity

to the current coastline and in the neighboring territory, and also with the help of data from the numerous archaeological excavations carried out in this area, has a plausible reconstruction of this stretch of the coastline been proposed. This substantially confirms the description handed down to us by Seneca (fig. 39).
The portion of the lava promontory on which ancient Pompeii was built, between the Marine Gate and the Stabian Gate, appears almost vertical and represents a section of an ancient coastal cliff. This can be seen both in the northern section of the Sarno plain, from Herculaneum to Oplontis, and in Pompeii itself, and in the southern section, from the zone of Pioppaino to Stabiae. This cliff owes its configuration to the maximum inland retreat of the coastline, as a consequence of the rise in sea level that occurred during the last interglacial period, known as the Holocene (between fifteen thousand and

50

five thousand years ago). This activity caused the sea to erode cliffs, both at the base of the Pompeian hillside and at the base of the alluvial deposits in the area of Castellammare di Stabia-Gragnano. It becomes clear that the presence of a more or less continuous cliff from Herculaneum to Stabiae had a considerable impact on the settlements that arose in this part of the territory. In particular the residential villas looking out over the gulf probably were built in a dominant position, overlooking the beach and the sea, at the edge of the cliff's vertical wall, which was now cut off from the sea but still near the coast.

A shift in the opposite direction occurred with the seaward advance of the coastline, when the rate of the sea level rising dropped below the rate of materials being deposited from Somma-Vesuvius and from the Lattari Mountains, transported by the Sarno and other streams. Thereafter beach deposits accumulated to create the first coastal sandbar. Identified in the area of Messigno, this sandbar is nearly rectilinear and parallel to the current coastline, datable between 5,600 and 4,500 years ago. The gradual lowering of the plain, tied both to the variation in the sea level and to volcanic-tectonic phenomena, led to a subsequent advancement of the coastline, with the formation of a secondary coastal bar, identified along the area between Bottaro and Pioppaino, with more modest evidence in the direction of

Stabiae (3,600–2,500 years ago). This was made up of black sand of aeolic origin, resting on ancient beach deposits. At the time of the eruption these deposits were inactive and were partially covered in the more depressed areas by the alluvial sediments of the Sarno. Later the second bar also was deactivated, and in the first century A.D. the area between the two sandy shores became the site of coastal bogs, due to the surfacing of the water table and the overflow of river waters during periods of flooding. However, dry areas (Messigno) persisted, where the remains of buildings and three stands of cypress have been discovered, buried by eruptive materials from Vesuvius. The trees were planted in Roman times, to reclaim lands rich in water and to demarcate farmland.

Thus in the first century A.D. the coastline was further advanced, with the formation of new sandy beaches, probably edged by pine forests, some hundred meters before the second coastal bar of Bottaro-Pioppaino. The coastline moreover created an indentation, corresponding to the bay or lagoon mentioned by Seneca, where the maritime port for the ancient city of Pompeii (in the area of Bottaro) probably was located; it also created the mouth of the Sarno River, further south (fig. 40). Finally, again along this section of the coast, farther north with regard to the bay or lagoon and near the marshy area, were salt-work installations that were of fundamental importance for the production of *garum*[1] also

[1] Ancient Roman type of fish-based sauce

41. Pompeii, Street of the Tombs, between the Villa of Diomedes and the Herculaneum Gate (photo early 1900s).

mentioned by Columella (*De re rustica* X, 130–136). Climate studies have shown that the sea level has gone down about 4 meters in the last two thousand years in the area of Vesuvius, due in part to the emptying of the magmatic chamber of Vesuvius after the eruption, and in part to the general lowering that affected the entire Tyrrhenian area.

42a. Pompeii, panorama from the Tower of Mercury (photo G. Sommer, late 1800s).

The Hill of Pompeii

A hilly area was chosen as the site for the primitive settlement —a lava spur elevated 30–35 meters above sea level, on the plain crossed by the Sarno. There was fertile soil, a rich water supply, and the promise of a better microclimate and drier lands, as well as greater ease in building enclosures and defenses. Moreover the proximity of the coast, approximately 1 kilometer from the built-up area, the presence of extensive salt works, and the navigable Sarno River were decisive factors for the city's economic and cultural development. In Roman times it became an important and wealthy commercial center along the axis road that linked Naples (Neapolis) and Nuceria. The developed area slopes sharply from north to south, toward the gulf, and the only flat area is the zone of the Forum and its neighboring districts. The perimeter of the walls, which have not yet been entirely uncovered, runs along the edges of the lava spur and is 3,200 meters long, enclosing an area of approximately 63.5 hectares. This area was not completely urbanized and, according to various hypotheses, was occupied during its final period of life by between 6,400 and 20,000 inhabitants (figs. 41, 42 a–b). The city has a "Hippodameic" layout, subdivided into regular lots formed by the intersection at right angles of two *decumani* running from east to west (Via Nolana and Via dell'Abbondanza) with three *cardines* running from north to south (Via Mercurio/Via delle Scuole, Via Stabiana, Via Nuceria). The lots thus

42b. Pompeii, Forum area (photo G. Sommer, late 1800s).

43a. Pompeii, street intersection near the Temple of Fortuna Augusta (photo G. Sommer, late 1800s).

43b. Pompeii, Large Theater (Anonymous, late 1800s, watercolor sketch).

43c. Pompeii, Amphitheater (Anonymous, late 1800s, watercolor sketch).

delimited were in turn subdivided by narrower streets into rectangular blocks. This layout was linked, with certain irregularities, to the primitive core of the city.

The city fabric did not clearly differentiate between elite, working-class, and commercial areas, while the public buildings were centered essentially in the areas of the Civil Forum, the Theater District, and the Amphitheater (figs. 43 a-b-c). The rocky outcroppings along the escarpments of the hill and their immediate vicinity were used to extract stone for public and private construction. The use of blocks of volcanic stone was particularly significant; these were used to pave the streets of the ancient city, and they came from a quarry

identified near the amphitheater. Small blocks of a reddish, spongy-looking lava also often were used for the *opus reticulatum* of the masonry for buildings. This material may have been extracted from the sides of the hill during the leveling of the summit, which was carried out to ready the area for settlement. This lava, so blistered that it looked like petrified sponge, is the most typical Pompeian volcanic rock. It is known as *cruma* and was mentioned by Vitruvius as *spongia sive pumex Pompeianus* [Pompeian sponge or pumice] (*De Architectura* II 6, 2).

As for the nature of the Pompeian hill, an earlier hypothesis proposed that it was formed from the accumulation of lava flows from Vesuvius,

44. Herculaneum, boundary of the part of the city that has been uncovered, with a section of the Decumanus Maximus.

which, following the same path repeatedly, built up one on top of another. However recent studies have shown that it is made up of the remains of an ancient volcanic edifice. In fact, morphologically the Pompeian region is formed from a series of low hills, which derive from an ancient crater centered in the current area of Fossa di Valle, and which thrust southward as far as the area of the hill of S. Abbondio. Recent studies have shown that the areas immediately below the lava wall, making up the ancient cliff, were covered at the time of the eruption by soil of an ashy composition, formed from predominantly sandy deposits. Within these deposits numerous man-made fragments were discovered.

This has led to the hypothesis that these areas, delimited by the marshy zones that developed between the low ridges of Messigno and Bottaro, were utilized by the inhabitants as dumping grounds.

THE PROMONTORY OF HERCULANEUM

This city [Herculaneum] is situated on an eminent promontory near the sea, with small walls, between two rivers, opposite Vesuvius; having crossed the river, which after Herculaneum, emptied into the sea... (SISENNA, *Historiarum*, IV, 53-54).
Hercules...founded a small city in the place where his ships were anchored, a city that took his name and that now is inhabited by the Romans, located between

Naples and Pompeii, and endowed with a safe port in all seasons (DIONYSIUS OF HALICARNASSUS, *Antiquitates Romanae*, I, 44, 1).
Near Naples is the stronghold of Herculaneum, with its promontory jutting out into the sea, beaten to such an amazing extent by the winds of the scirocco, that a healthy environment is created (STRABO, *Geography*, V, 4, 8, C 246–247).

Sisenna, Dionysius of Halicarnassus, and Strabo provide us with some brief but informative descriptions of the city of Herculaneum, which have been substantially confirmed by the most recent archaeological finds. Indeed, the ancient city, only a small portion of which has been uncovered, was erected on a high promontory, about twenty meters above sea level, which was made up of volcanic tuff and bordered at the sides by the waterways mentioned by Sisenna (fig. 44). At least in the central section, at a lower level, a so-called suburban quarter jutted out toward sea. This area consisted of a monumental bath facility and a sacred zone with twelve barrel vaults below, facing directly out over the beach. These were probably used as storage for boats, as well as for multistory dwellings (fig. 45). As has already been observed in the case of ancient Pompeii, the city was established in a salubrious location, due to its optimum exposure to the southwest winds and its proximity to the sea. It could also be easily defended from external attack.

The area to the west of the city,

45. Herculaneum, sacred area of the Suburban Quarter and central section of the inhabited area, with Cardo IV.

the focus of the most recent excavations, has revealed the presence of a deep valley between the inhabited area and the suburban Villa of the Papyri. Here one may find one of the two water courses mentioned by Sisenna, as well as an unexpected extension of the city for more than 40 meters seaward from the coastline that was known to have been near the suburban quarter. This might provide the first archaeological indication of the existence of a more extensive port area, a feature that is mentioned in the passage by Dionysius of Halicarnassus but has heretofore been ignored.

In the portion of the city that has been uncovered, the layout of the populated area, organized according to a rectangular "Hippodameic" scheme, slopes down toward the sea (fig. 46). The stretch of coastline near the area of Herculaneum inhabited prior to the eruption of A.D. 79 has been reconstructed on the basis of excavations carried out in recent decades, particularly beneath the suburban quarter. In fact, deposits comprising the ancient beach of Herculaneum have been discovered approximately 4.2 meters beneath the current sea level. These comprise three levels: volcanic tuff, black sand, and gravel. The latter is covered by a fine layer of ash, which was deposited in the first pyroclastic surge that demolished the city during the eruption of 79.

A layer of tuff, surfacing in the area directly northwest of the coast, probably originated from flows of pyroclastic materials from an unknown eruption of Somma. It represents the most ancient level on the beach and constitutes the principal terrace structure upon which the ancient city was constructed. The zone of the ancient beach where the tuff is exposed has a flat surface, due to the erosive action of the sea. A series of parallel fissures run perpendicular to the city, caused by surf activity and the incursion of sea waves onto the tuffaceous plane.

The second level consists of black sand, located immediately above the bank of tuff. It is probably derived from the erosion of volcanic rocks, and numerous shells of sea organisms were found within it during the excavations of the early 1980s. Granulometric analyses carried out on this sand have shown that in color and composition it is similar to the present-day sand near the Vesuvian coast.

The uppermost level of the beach prior to the A.D. 79 eruption consists of a gravelly deposit of limestone and lava pebbles, as well as fragments of brick and various other materials from the populated area, in a thin layer of blackish sand. It is interesting to note that the fragments appear rounded and in some cases flattened in the lower portion of the gravel level, while they are angular in the upper portion. This differentiation within the same deposit is due to the varying wave action of the surf, which has affected only the lower level. It allows us to discriminate this upper layer from the two other layers, whose interruption is tied to the sea level at the moment of the eruption. In fact, it is plausible to hypothesize that the rising of the soil in the area of Herculaneum and in the entire region of Vesuvius resulted

46. Herculaneum, section of Cardo IV between Insulae III and IV.

from the ascent of the magma toward the surface. This widespread rise reduced the effects of the surf on the beach; only the lower portion of the gravelly deposit was subject to erosion. The presence of brick and other building materials within the gravel level shows that at least part of the beach was used as a dumping ground, following the earthquakes that struck the area of Vesuvius between A.D. 62 and 79 (in particular beneath the House of Aristides, where an accumulation of domestic painted plaster was discovered).

THE STABIAN SITE

Stabiae developed over the broad plateau of the hill of Varano, at the base of the Lattari Mountains, at a height of approximately 50 meters above sea level, in a panoramic position overlooking the Bay of Naples. Nothing is known of its urban layout.

Ancient Stabiae, an important commercial center with a seaport, openly sided against Rome during the Social War. Like the more important centers of Pompeii and Herculaneum, it was conquered in 89 B.C. by Silla's army and lost all administrative and political autonomy.

During the excavations undertaken by the Bourbons during the 1700s, numerous urban remains were discovered in the eastern sector of the Varano plateau. As was customary in that period, however, these were immediately covered over again, after the removal of all the frescoes, floors, and the domestic furnishings that were considered most interesting and valuable. However thanks to a blueprint drawn up by Swiss engineer Karl Weber in 1759, we can distinguish a cluster of buildings, consisting of *tabernae*, residences, and a square with a portico on at least two sides, as well as some intersecting paved streets. These have been unanimously identified as a section of ancient Stabiae. On the basis of this partial but valuable evidence, excavations have not been resumed in this part of the Varano plateau. It is practically impossible to define the precise nature and extent of this urban arrangement prior to the A.D. 79 eruption. However, according to some recent hypotheses, we can perhaps identify, at least in part, a permanent market used by the local population for buying and selling goods and products of the region.

Moreover on the Varano plateau and in particular on the northern side that juts out over the sea, six large residential villas have been discovered, including the famous Villa Ariadne and the Villa San Marco. These provide evidence that beginning in the first century B.C., this area was famous for its healthy climate and for the excellence of the waters, and that it was much in favor with wealthy Roman society (fig. 47).

Communication between the settlements on the plateau and the coast below was ensured by a flat ramp, subterranean in places, bending sharply back and forth along the escarpment near the Villa Ariadne. There was probably also a connecting tunnel carved into the rock (Grotta S. Biagio).

Finally it is hypothesized that at the base of the hill, along the coast, there was a port area with a small related settlement. It is here that Pliny the Elder may have disembarked in the late afternoon of August 24, A.D. 79, to stay with his friend Pomponianus, who resided in a nearby villa.

URBANIZATION OF THE AREA

The exploitation of natural resources that the Vesuvian region had to offer was decisive for intense human habitation and had a profound effect on the area's appearance. Thanks to the Tabula Peutingeriana (a road map from the twelfth or thirteenth century, which reproduces an original map dating back perhaps to the time of Augustus) (fig. 48), and to finds uncovered in the region, we can affirm that in the first century B.C. the entire area was served by a broad network of roads. The main axis was the road that linked Nuceria to Naples and to the important

seaport of Puteoli (Pozzuoli). After a bridge was built over the Sarno River, this road continued on to Pompeii and Oplontis, present-day Torre Annunziata. Later, with the addition of a section between the coastline and the slopes of Vesuvius, the road reached Herculaneum. Near Oplontis there was a coastal road that broke away from the

47. Stabiae, Villa of San Marco, peristyle with central pool.

48. Tabula Peutingeriana, section between Herculaneum and Stabiae.

49. Pompeii, Herculaneum Gate (Anonymous, late 1800s, watercolor sketch).

Nuceria-Naples road. After passing *Salinae Herculae* and the seaport of Pompeii, situated on a spit of land between the marsh area and the sea inlet, it continued onward, proceeding by the mouth of the Sarno toward Stabiae. Pompeii, on the other hand, was connected to Stabiae by two other roads. The first ran straight from the Stabian Gate, while the second began at the Marine Gate, then headed toward the seaport, joining up with the aforementioned coastal road from Oplontis. Two inscriptions have been discovered, the first in the Oscan language, datable to 89 B.C., the second in Latin, that refer to the *veru sarinu* and *Porta Salis*, what we now call the Herculaneum Gate (fig. 49). This evidence allows us to confirm with certainty the existence of a direct connecting road between the city and the salt-work facilities located further to the southwest along the coast.

Moreover a connecting road outside the city linked up with the extra-urban road network, allowing vehicular traffic heading towards other sites in Campania to avoid entering the city. However we have no information that would allow us to reconstruct the principal road system to the northeast of the city, or the dense network of secondary roads that must have served the entire Vesuvius region. The two large cities of Pompeii and Herculaneum developed in this area; Pompeii became a site of intense commercial traffic, tied to local products and flourishing crafts, while Herculaneum was more residential and gravitated toward Naples.

The small city of Stabiae was located on the Varano plateau, built on the ashes of the town destroyed by Silla's army during the Social War. Oplontis, a group of residential villas with waystation facilities for travelers, was located in the immediate vicinity of Pompeii at a distance of approximately 5 kilometers. It had baths and a hotel, as well as storage facilities for the agricultural products of the neighboring territory.

Two monumental buildings, called Villa A and Villa B, have come to light in Oplontis. The owners of Villa A have been identified as the *Gens Poppaea*, to which Sabina, second wife of Nero, belonged; Villa B's owner has been identified as Lucius Crassius Tertius.

The identity of the owner of Villa A is entirely hypothetical, based on a painted inscription on an amphora, addressed to *Secundus*, a freedman who had belonged to Sabina Poppaea. There is more concrete proof for the last owner of the Villa B complex, thanks to the discovery of a bronze seal with the name *L. Crassius Tertius* (fig. 50).

However the great thickness of volcanic material from the eruption of 79 and later lava flows (over 20 meters deep in all) have left us with scant information for reconstructing the diversity of the region of Herculaneum, with the exception of some residential villas along the coastline (Villa Sora and the so-called Palaestra Baths in present-day Torre del Greco). Finally with regard to the region of Pompeii, we have evidence that has allowed us to identify two more dense concentrations of buildings, conventionally known as the "Seaport" and the "River Port." These are neither mentioned specifically in classical sources nor indicated in the Tabula Peutingeriana.

Excavations carried out in the late 1800s and early 1900s brought to light numerous building remains in the area of Bottaro (figs. 51–52), the sector

50. Oplontis, Villa A; portico n. 34 with the garden in front.

Oplontis by the coast road; it was characterized by waystations and loading facilities for ships'cargo. This activity was of vital importance for the Pompeian economy, as Strabo mentions. In one passage, he explicitly maintains that *Pompeii… functioned as a port for Nola, Nuceria, and Acerrae* (*Geography* V, 4, 8), thus confirming the city's important role as a principal center for the collection and sorting of goods going into and out of the Campanian hinterland.

Certain passages in Cicero (*Ad Atticum* XIV, 20, 1, 2, 3; XVI, 3, 6, 7, 8) may also refer to the existence of a seaport area. He mentions his frequent stays at a villa that he owned, in the vicinity of Pompeii:
I went by boat from my Pompeian villa to our Lucullus's retreat; I wrote this when I was about to

51. Pompeii, area of Bottaro. Workshops discovered during the Fienga excavations in the 1930s.

overlooking the bay or lagoon, with the salt works to the north, the mouth of the Sarno to the south, and marshland behind. This location has been identified unanimously as a seaport, connected to Pompeii and

52. Pompeii, fresco. Imaginary maritime landscape with structures along the coast (MANN, Inv. No. 9482).

embark from my villa in Pompeii; I wrote these things while navigating toward my villa in Pompeii.

This area also was the site of intense fishing activity that, along with the salt produced at the nearby *Salinae Herculae*, provided the essential ingredients for the renowned *garum*, a sauce made from fish brine, which was another pillar of the flourishing and active Pompeian economy. This port area, the size of which remains unknown, had an administrative structure obviously subordinate to that of Pompeii, and it probably was also the heart of the *Pagus Augustus Felix Suburbanus*, the name given to the centuriated territories distributed to veterans of Silla's victorious army. These veterans, along with their families, settled on these lands at the founding of the Pompeii colony (*Colonia Cornelia Veneria Pompeianorum*), after the Social War and the related distribution of confiscated assets to the victors.

The "river port" (fig. 53) was probably smaller but still of great importance to the area's economy. It was built near the mouth of the Sarno River, on the right bank, near an important road that, starting at the Stabian Gate, linked Pompeii directly to the Stabian area.

The current state of research has shown that the port was made up of storage buildings, some of which have been restored, and bath facilities that were under construction at the time of the eruption. The river's navigability was noted by Strabo: *its course is utilized to import and export goods* (*Geography* V, 4, 8), and this made the river port a strategic point for handling products both

53. Murecine, hospitium with triclinium b (Pompeii). This area was the site of the discovery of numerous structures related to the "River Port" on the Sarno, including a building for guests, identified as a *hospitium*, or inn.

54-55. Pompeii, frescoes. Imaginary views of residential villas. (MANN, Inv. No. 9406).

from the hinterlands and from the nearby seaport.

The healthy climate, the beauty of the gulf landscape, and the decision of the Julio-Claudian emperors to reside in areas like Capreae (Capri) and Baiae (Baia) contributed decisively to the fortunes of the area. Indeed, the region became so thick with vacation villas near the sea that it seemed as if the entire coastline, from Cape Misenum as far as Punta Campanella, was made up of a single city: *and the entire gulf is studded, in part*

56. Boscoreale, country villa of Pisanella. View of the wine cellar at the time of the excavations in the late 1800s.

by cities that I have mentioned and in part by villas and farms, without interruption, to the extent that it seems to have the appearance of a single city (STRABO, *Geography* V, 4, 8). Because of their size and the refinement of their decorative programs, the six villas discovered at the ridge of the Varano hill in Stabiae, Villa A of Oplontis, Villa Sora near Torre del Greco, and the Villa of the Papyri in Herculaneum provide clear examples of what wealthy residences of the time looked like along the coast of the Bay of Naples (figs. 54–55).
If we move inland, the building typology changes radically. The luxury seaside villa, clearly residential in nature, is transformed into a rustic villa, characterized by spaces and structures suitable for growing and preserving products from the fertile soil of the Vesuvian region. The density of this type of construction is well documented, both in the Sarno

plain, particularly in the vicinity of the present-day town of Scafati, and along the slopes of the Lattari Mountains. Another specific concentration of buildings has been verified between Pompeii and the slopes of Vesuvius, particularly in the area of Boscoreale and Terzigno, where some important examples of farms devoted predominantly to vine cultivation have been brought to light (fig. 56).
In addition to the prosperity generated by the exchange of goods and by the widespread presence of residential buildings, especially along the coastline, the wealth and fame of the Vesuvian region were also based on the fertility of the soil in these flatlands, which terminated in high ridges near the slopes of Vesuvius and the Lattari Mountains. As mentioned earlier, we have less information about farm production in the area of Herculaneum. This is due to the scarcity of information in

57. Pompeii, House of the Vettii. Fresco depicting wine-cupids (early 1900s, lithograph with watercolor).

ancient texts, the lack of consistent discoveries in the region because of the great depth of the volcanic deposits, and the small portion of the city, which in any case seems to be overwhelmingly residential, that has been uncovered.

We have more information regarding the Pompeian area, and putting the various pieces together has allowed us to satisfactorily reconstruct the economic productivity of this region.

The cultivation of vines was extremely important (fig. 57), as attested to in numerous ancient texts, by the aforementioned fresco depicting Dionysus near Vesuvius, and by many excavations in the area, including part of a small vineyard near Villa Regina in Boscoreale. Such vineyards covered a good part of the region, particularly the slopes of Vesuvius, as numerous ancients attested. Columella: (*The vines*) *cover the very famous slopes of Vesuvius and Surrentum*[2] (*De re rustica* III, 2, 10); Martial: *Here is Vesuvius, once shady with green vine leaves, here are vats dripping with the sap of prized grapes: these the cliffs of dear Bacchus* (*Epigrammata* IV, 44); Florus: *Here the vine-clad mountains, Gaurus, Falernus, Massicus, and loveliest of all, Vesuvius* (*Epitome* I, 11, 3-6); and finally Cassius Dio: *The high parts of that mountain are covered with many trees and vines* (*Hist. Rom.* LXVI, 21–23).

But a passage by Pliny the Elder is especially useful for identifying the various species of vines, such as the *Vennuncula* vine, that were planted in the small vineyards, yielding a variety of products. *The Vennuncula* (*vine*), *one of the*

58. Pompeii, House of A. Umbricius Scaurus. Mosaic depicting a typical clay vessa for *garum* (SAP, Inv. No. 15188).

59. Pompeii, Fullonica VI, 8, 20. Fresco with a depiction of the phases of texile production (MANN, Inv. No. 9773).

² Sorrento

68

species that flourishes best and whose wine is most suitable to being preserved in jars, is called Surcula by the Campanians, Scapola by others, Numisiana in Terracina… its wine, sealed in amphorae, in the area of Sorrento as far as Vesuvius, is extremely robust (Nat. Hist. XIV, 34–35). Writing of the Murgentina vine, he states: *There, in fact, the Murgentina, from Sicily, dominates. Some call it Pompeian, and it flourishes above all in fertile territories (Nat. Hist. XIV, 34–35).* In the same passage, Pliny writes about the *Holconia* or *Horconia* vine, which takes its name from the powerful Pompeian family, the *Holconii.* In addition to viticulture, salt works along the coastline made possible a thriving and valued production of *garum,* the famous condiment of the Roman era, made by steeping fish, particularly mackerel and tuna, in large vessels of seawater brine, which were then exposed to the sun.

Pompeian *garum* (fig. 58), mentioned by Pliny the Elder, was known for its high quality (*Nat. Hist.* XXXI, 94): *Clazomenae, Pompeii, and Leptis also were famous for their garum,* which was a source of wealth for certain families in Pompeii. First among them were the *Umbricii,* veritable industrialists in this field, who found an unusual way to publicize their trade: the decorative mosaics of the floor of the atrium of their house, at the corners of the *impluvium,* include a depiction of clay *garum* containers.

There was also a significant olive industry, and Cato writes that Pompeii was where olive presses were produced and sold (*De Agricultura* XXII, 3; CXXXV, 2).

Finally, extensive parts of the region, in addition to supporting the cultivation of grains and various types of vegetables, including the renowned Pompeian cabbage (COLUMELLA, *De re rustica,* X, 130-136), were used for sheep farming. A passage by Seneca, related to the earthquake of A.D. 62, mentions the extent of such activity. (*Nat. quaest.,* VI, 27, 1: *We already have mentioned that a flock of six hundred sheep perished in the region of Pompeii*), and the area around Pompeii was full of workshops dedicated to the working of raw wool and sheepskins and their transformation into finished products (fig. 59).

Portentous Events
between A.D. 62 and 79

PREFACE

The period from A.D. 62 to 79 has yielded literary, epigraphic, and iconographic testimonials and numerous instances of building restoration that were in progress before the eruption have been identified. These provide significant information about earthquakes that occurred in the Vesuvian area, which, considered volcanic rather than tectonic in origin, can be seen as some of the most important events foreshadowing the eruption. Taken as a whole, these data make it possible to isolate two events that had considerable impact on buildings and inhabitants, in A.D. 62 and 64, and to verify the presence of continuous seismic instability that particularly affected the area around Vesuvius. However, these manifestations, noted and recorded in sources during Roman times, were clearly not understood by the ancients as being linked to the familiar mountain.

THE EARTHQUAKE OF A.D. 62

The event of greatest intensity, which caused extensive damage to structures in the settlement and upset the life of the inhabitants in this flourishing section of Campania, occurred on February 5, A.D. 62. Seneca begins Book VI of his *Naturales*

Quaestiones with a description of the Vesuvian earthquake. While not comprehensive, his testimony still provides us with some important information for reconstructing the consequences of this violent seismic jolt: *Pompeii… is ruined due to an earthquake, and the neighboring territories also have been upset, in the winter months in addition, which our ancestors reputed to be usually immune from such risk. This earthquake occurred on February 5, during the consulate of Regulus and Virginius, and it devastated Campania with considerable damage, never safe from such calamity, unscathed however and often only terrified. Much of the city of Herculaneum also was ruined and the buildings that were saved are in danger. The colony of Nuceria did not suffer losses but is not without damage. Naples also lost many private residences but not public buildings and was only moderately touched by greater disaster; but some villas collapsed, others here and there were struck without being damaged. Other calamities must be added to these: they say that a flock of some hundred sheep was destroyed, statues were broken, some of the people remained confused and later wandered through the territory, incapable of helping themselves…*(Nat. quaest. VI, 1, 1-3); *…we should pay no*

60. Pompeii, Temple of Isis (G. Gigante, late nineteenth century, color lithograph).

heed to those who have written off Campania and who emigrated after this event and maintain that they will never again set foot in that region... (*Nat. quaest.* VI, 1, 10); *For this reason it is believed that the islands have more stabile soil and that the closer cities are to the sea, the safer they are. Pompeii and Herculaneum have proven the groundlessness of this opinion* (*Nat. quaest.* VI, 26, 3–4); *In this earthquake in Campania there moreover occurred certain singular facts, which must be taken into account. We have already mentioned that a flock of six hundred sheep perished in the region of Pompeii* (*Nat. quaest.* VI, 27, 1).

In Tacitus we find other news about the destructive quake of 62, limited, however, to the city of Pompeii: *an earthquake ruined much of Pompeii, celebrated city of Campania* (*Annales* XV, 22).

Moreover it is unanimously agreed that two famous marble bas-reliefs, located in the *lararium* of the House of Lucius Caecilius Iucundus in Pompeii (V, 1, 26) and three inscriptions, one discovered in Pompeii and two in Herculaneum, are related to this event. The Pompeian inscription (CIL X 846), datable to A.D. 62–68, attests to the complete rebuilding of the Temple of Isis (fig. 60), dedicated to the divinity of Egyptian origin who was much venerated in the city. The rebuilding was carried out at the expense of Numerius Popidius Celsinus' father, Numerius Popidius Ampliatus, who secured his six-year-old son's future entry into political life with this donation (*aedes Isidis terrae motu conlapsa*).

The first relevant inscription in Herculaneum (CIL X 1406), dating back to A.D. 76, refers to the allocation of public funds by the Emperor Vespasian for the restoration of the Temple of the Mother of the Gods. We do not know the exact location of the building site, but assume that it probably was in the immediate vicinity of the Palaestra, since the inscription was discovered within its ash deposits (*templum Matris Deum terrae motu conlapsum restituit*).

The second Herculanean inscription, which is extremely fragmentary, can be dated to A.D. 75–76. According to the proposed words that have been filled in, based on the similar first inscription, it refers to restoration work on an unknown monument in the populated area (*Herculane [i terrae motu collapsum? restituit]*).

Finally the two bas-reliefs, one from the House of Lucius Caecilius Iucundus and the other from the immediate vicinity, provide a realistic if unrefined image of the effects of the quake on certain public buildings in Pompeii (figs. 61–62). The first depicts the *Capitolium*, the city's most important temple, in the Forum area, with columns on the façade, two equestrian statues on the steps, and a triumphal arch flanking it to the west, all slanting to one side, emphasizing the effects of the seismic vibrations. In the second bas-relief we can identify the Vesuvian Gate, tilting strongly toward one side, between the *Castellum Aquae* and a section of the city's enclosing wall.

However we do not feel that we can relate this disastrous event to the numerous restoration projects underway in Vesuvian residences at the time of the eruption. More realistically, these may have been ongoing in order to rebuild masonry structures and decorative elements damaged by intense seismic activity that took place during the subsequent seventeen-year period, between the earthquake of 62 and the eruption of 79. This span of time is too long to have been spent merely restoring private buildings. It can only be explained by property owners

61–62. Pompeii, House of Caecilius Iucundus. Bas-relief depicting the effects of the earthquake of A.D. 62 in Pompeii (SAP Inv. No. 20470; MCR Inv. No. 1368).

moving, even if temporarily, while they not only repaired damage that had occurred, but also rebuilt spaces to improve the habitability of their houses or to adapt them to new economic activities.

As for interventions in public buildings, it is more plausible that these projects, due to their greater complexity and high cost, took more time. Thus it is likely, as the two Herculanean inscriptions also record, that in A.D. 79 or in the years immediately preceding, work was still underway to repair the damage inflicted by the quake of 62, which was perhaps further aggravated by later events. It is also possible that restoration work had just been completed. This information taken as a whole allows us to attempt a reconstruction of the intensity and effects of this seismic shock, which, in terms of the long life of the volcano, can be considered an interval between an inactive phase and the beginning of the new phase that culminated in the eruption of A.D. 79.

The fundamental passage by Seneca, around which all other information revolves, lists in succession the cities struck by the quake, with a brief but significant commentary for each, depending on the severity of the damages suffered: Pompeii, Herculaneum, Nuceria, Naples. All the evidence in our possession verifies the great damage sustained by buildings in the cities of Pompeii and Herculaneum. This allows us to hypothesize that the epicenter of the earthquake, characterized by low to medium energy (a magnitude of about 5 on the Richter scale), with a focus close to the surface (5–6

kilometers in depth), must have been located in the vicinity of these inhabited areas. The quake's most destructive effects also affected the other settlements along the slopes of the volcano, in a rather limited area. Moreover it has been estimated that the intensity of the jolt for Pompeii must have been no greater than eight degrees on the MCS scale of earthquake intensity, while for Herculaneum it must have been between seven and eight degrees. Nuceria and Naples, however, being farther from the epicenter, were struck less intensely, with a jolt that has been estimated to be no greater than seven degrees on the MCS scale.

An event of such magnitude had an extremely violent impact on the cities of Vesuvius, with the collapse of monumental, public, and sacred buildings: in Pompeii, the Basilica (fig. 63), the *Capitolium*, and the Temple of Isis, and in Herculaneum, the Temple of the Mother of the Gods. There must have been innumerable victims throughout the area, although the sources in our possession do not mention this expressly in their itemization of the consequences. They do, however, mention that part of the population wandered the countryside, terrorized. Nevertheless if we look at Seneca's passage about the city of Nuceria, using a debated translation of *ut sine clade* as *without loss of human lives*, we have an implicit admission that in Pompeii and Herculaneum there were victims, if not in great numbers.

Finally, to complete the picture of the effects of such a destructive earthquake, we

should remember, again using Seneca as a reference, that some of the inhabitants of the area who moved away were fearful about returning to the region after the quake.

Thus there is no question that there must have been immediate and profound changes in the social and economic life of the area. Only with the passage of years did things slowly return to normal, although with a heightened level of tension due to continued seismic activity.

SEISMIC ACTIVITY BETWEEN A.D. 62 AND 79

In fact Campania did not cease experiencing repeated tremors, with some rather weak jolts, but with serious damage, as buildings, already shaken, were shaken anew *and, resting in a state of precarious balance, needed not a decisive push but merely a tremble to fall. (Nat. quaest.* VI, 31, 1).

Thus Seneca recalls a series of jolts that occurred after the event of February 5, 62, demonstrating the long-term instability of the area already affected by the quake.

Two years later, in A.D. 64, a second earthquake struck Campania. This event entered official historic records because it involved the emperor Nero, who was visiting the city of Naples. Two well-known passages by Suetonius and Tacitus refer to the earthquake:

He had his debut in Naples and, notwithstanding the fact that the theater shook because of a sudden earthquake jolt, he continued to sing until he reached the end of the 63. Pompeii, Basilica. Interior of the hall with the colonnade as it was discovered at the time of the excavations in the early 1800s. The building, severely damaged after the earthquake of A.D. 62, was in the process of being restored when the eruption took place (photo G Sommer, late 1800s).

piece he had begun (*Vita Neronis,* XX, 2); *something happened there that most considered ill-omened, but Nero, instead, saw as providential and a sign of divine favor: as soon as the spectators left, the empty theater collapsed without harm to anyone* (*Annales* XV, 34, 1).

We also must add to these sources a painted wall inscription (*CIL* IV, No. 3822), discovered in Pompeii. It honors Nero, and the text, *pro salute Ner[onis],* can be interpreted as a celebration of the emperor's escape from danger during his performance in the theater in Naples. Another inscription discovered in Naples (*CIL* X, No. 1481) and datable to A.D. 80–81, which mentions restoration work carried out by the emperor Titus on important public buildings in the city, uses the word "earthquake" in the plural (*terrae motibus*). This might refer to rebuilding projects carried out in Naples both after the seismic shocks that accompanied the eruption of A.D. 79 and to those that occurred earlier. We have no other information about the quake of A.D. 64 that would allow us to estimate its intensity, the area affected by the event, or the resulting effects on buildings and the resident population. However, understanding this earthquake in light of the changed dynamics of the volcano, we can hypothesize that in the more strictly defined Vesuvian area, buildings did suffer further damage, although we cannot calculate the extent. The absence of specific sources until the eruption of A.D. 79 is in part compensated by the contribution of archaeological data provided by the excavation of the cities of Pompeii, Herculaneum, and

other settlements in areas neighboring the volcano. Innumerable examples of restoration work have been found in the masonry, and the presence of construction work in many buildings at the time of the eruption may relate, at least in part, to repairs necessitated by widespread seismic activity in the area, over the period between A.D. 64 and 79.

Moreover Pliny the Younger himself, describing the terrible conflagration of Vesuvius, does not refer to a clearly specified event but does provide us with essential testimony about the frequency of earthquakes in Campania: *Earlier, for the duration of many days, the earth had shaken, but this fact did not cause fear, because earthquakes are a commonly observed phenomenon in Campania* (*Epistulae* VI, 20). The totality of archaeological data and the significant testimony of Pliny furthermore allow us to suggest that numerous private residences, after restoration work and the intensification of seismic activity in the days preceding the eruption, probably were abandoned entirely or in part by their owners. Finally, it is interesting to stress that the picture reconstructed from contemporary accounts is analogous to what was observed recently, on the occasion of the reawakening of certain volcanoes, such as Mount St. Helens, Pinatubo, and El Chicón. These eruptions were all preceded by a series of portentous phenomena and in particular by an increase in seismic activity during the two months prior to the eruption, confined to the area of the volcanoes, with depths no greater than a few kilometers.

The Eruption

Preface

The eruption of Vesuvius in A.D. 79 was one of the most famous and significant in the volcanological history of the world. The two letters that Pliny the Younger sent to the historian Tacitus in A.D. 106 (*Epist.* VI 16, 20) are an important and dramatic account of what happened during the days of August 24 and 25, A.D. 79, and they can be considered the first documents of modern volcanology.

The first letter describes the voyage that Pliny the Elder undertook along the Vesuvian coast, to follow the eruptive phenomena from a close vantage point. He then landed in Stabiae, where he died, as described in the second recounting of events as experienced by Pliny the Younger in Misenum. A description of the voyage (fig. 64) and the circumstances of the famous naturalist's death were later handed down by friends of Pomponianus to Pliny the Elder's nephew, Pliny the Younger, who collected them in a letter sent many years later to Tacitus. Additional information is

64. Reconstruction of the voyage made by Pliny the Elder along the Vesuvian coast, on the afternoon of August 24, A.D. 79, before arriving in Stabiae.

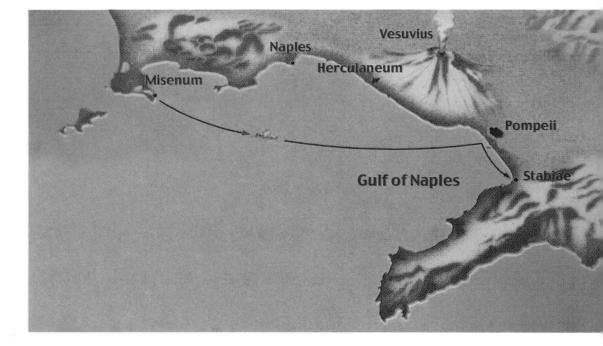

contained in a passage by Cassius Dio, which, though written over a century later, still gives us additional data, particularly for reconstructing the early phases of the eruption.

The integration of ancient sources with archaeological finds and volcanological data that have emerged from stratigraphic studies have made it possible to reconstruct the chronology of events that took place during those days. This chronology is based particularly on two assumptions. First, the beginning of the paroxysmal phase began toward one o'clock in the afternoon on August 24, as indicated in Pliny's first letter (*hora fere septima*). Then, the surge that reached Stabiae, killing Pliny the Elder and forcing Pliny the Younger and those residing in Misenum to flee, which is the first event described in the second letter, began shortly after dawn on August 25, toward 8:00 in the morning.

Studies of volcanic deposits make it possible to establish that two important phases distinguish this eruption. The first, characterized by a dense rain of ash and pumice (fallout), affected a vast area southeast of the volcano, along the Pompeii-Stabiae route, covering the region with materials that varied in depth from some ten centimeters, slightly south of Herculaneum, to about 2.5–3 meters, in the hardest hit area, 10–15 kilometers from the center of emission. The second phase was characterized by the formation of a series of pyroclastic flows (surges and flows), which predominantly affected the areas south, west, and east of the volcano, depositing enormous quantities of pyroclastic materials, and causing tremendous destruction and the death of those who had no way to escape during the preceding hours.

An Account of the Eruption in Pliny's Two Letters

Letter VI, 16

Dear Tacitus,
You ask me to tell you about the death of my uncle, so that you might more accurately hand it down to posterity. And I am grateful to you: since I foresee that his death, if recounted by you, will be destined to lasting glory. Even if he in fact perished amidst the devastation of the most beautiful lands, along with entire populations and cities, under memorable circumstances, almost as if to survive forever in memory. And even if he himself composed many and enduring works, the immortality of your writings will add much to the duration of his fame. I consider quite fortunate those who are given the divine gift either to do things worthy of being told or to write things worthy of being read; those who are granted both gifts are fortunate indeed. My uncle will be among them, thanks to his works and to your own.

Thus it is even more willingly that I set about to complete what
you ask, indeed I look upon it as a kindness.

He was in Misenum and was commanding the fleet in person.
The ninth day before the calends of September,[1] toward the
seventh hour,[2] my mother pointed out to him a cloud, unusual
in its vastness and appearance. After taking a sun bath and then
a bath in cold water, he had a snack, lying down and studying;
he asked for his shoes, then climbed up to a place from which it
was possible to get a good look at this phenomenon. A cloud was
forming (to those who were looking at it from so far away, it
wasn't clear from which mountain it originated, later we knew
it was Vesuvius). Its appearance and shape would be best
expressed as being that of an umbrella pine. Since, stretched
upward like an extremely tall trunk, it then spread out like
branches. I think it first rose up, originating from a stream of
air, which then abated, so it gave way to its own weight,
spreading out slowly. Sometimes it was white, sometimes dirty
and blotchy, because of the soil or the ash that it carried.
Erudite person that he was, it seemed to him that the
phenomenon had to be observed better and from closer range. He
ordered a Liburnian galley to be prepared; he said I could go
with him if I so desired; I answered that I preferred to stay
behind to study, indeed by chance he had given me an
assignment. He was leaving the house when he received a note
from Rectina, wife of Caesius, frightened by the danger that
threatened (since her villa was at the foot of the mountain and
there was no way out except by boat). She implored to be rescued
from such a terrible situation. My uncle changed his plans and
what he had undertaken out of his love for science, which he
brought to an end out of a sense of duty. He put to sea the
quadriremes and embarked, to bring help not only to Rectina,
but also to many others, since being pleasantly located near the
beach, the area was very populated. He hurried to go from where
others were fleeing, he went straight there, steering toward a
place of danger, so without fear that he dictated and described
every phenomenon of that terrible scourge, every aspect, as it
appeared before his eyes.

Ash already was falling on the boats, much hotter and denser
that one would have guessed. Pumice and also blackened
pebbles, cooked and fractured by the fire. Then there was an
unexpected shoal and the beach was obstructed by masses hurled
from the mountain. He hesitated a moment, to see if he would
have to return, but then exclaimed to the pilot who was
exhorting him to do this: "Fortune helps the brave, head for
Pomponianus!" These people were in Stabiae, on the other side of
the gulf (since there the sea went inland, following the bank that
went along, gradually delineating a curve). There Pomponianus,
since the danger was not near, but in sight, however, and could
become imminent if it grew, had transported his things to some
boats, having decided to flee if the adverse wind died down. But

[1] August 24
[A.D. 79].
[2] between 2:00
and 3:00 in the
afternoon.

79

then this was entirely favorable to my uncle, who arrived, embraced his fearful friend, encouraged and comforted him, and, to clearly calm his fears, asked to be brought to the bath. He washed and happily dined, or even more impressively, feigned cheerfulness.

Soon great flames and vast fires shone from many points on Mount Vesuvius, the gleam and the light made more vivid by the nighttime shadows. To calm people's fears, my uncle said that these were burning fires, abandoned by fleeing farmers. Then he went to rest and fell into a genuine sleep. Those who kept watch from the threshold heard his breathing, made heavier and noisy by his great girth. But the courtyard through which one entered that apartment was already growing high with ash mixed with stones, so that had he lingered much longer in the room, he would no longer have been able to get out. Awakened, he left and reached Pomponianus and the others, who had not slept a wink. They discussed among themselves whether they should remain in a covered place or stay out in the open. Continuous and prolonged jolts of the earth shook the house, almost tearing it from its foundations, as it seemed to move up and down. On the other hand outside they feared the rain of stones, however light and porous. But faced with these dangers, he chose to go outside. But if he was motivated by reason, the others were ruled by fear. They put pillows over their heads, fastening them with sheets; this was their shelter against the rain of stones.

It was already daytime, but nighttime reigned, darker and deeper than any other, even if pierced by many fires and various lights. He wanted to go out on the beach and get a close view to see if it were possible to put out to sea. But the sea was still rough and impassable. There, resting upon a stretched out sheet, he asked again and again for cool water and drank it avidly. But then the flames and the smell of sulfur that preceded them put some people to flight but roused my uncle. Supported by two slaves, he stood up, but immediately fell down again, because, I suppose, the air, thickened with ash, had obstructed his breathing and blocked his windpipe, which was delicate and narrow by nature and frequently inflamed. When daylight returned (the third day after he had breathed his last), his body was found intact and unharmed, covered with the clothing he had been wearing. He seemed more like a man who was sleeping than one who was dead.

Meanwhile in Misenum, my mother and I ... but this has no bearing on the story, and you only want to know about his death. And so I will stop now. I only wish to add one thing: I immediately put down everything I witnessed and heard, when the memories were more truthful. You should take what is most important. Indeed it is one thing to write a letter, yet another to write history. It is one thing to write to a friend, another to write for the public. Farewell.

Letter VI, 20

Dear Tacitus,

Made curious by my letter that I wrote at your request, you have asked me about the death of my uncle. You want to know not only the fears, but also the dangers I faced, when I was left at Misenum (in fact I was about to tell you this but was interrupted).

Although my grief and pain are renewed and the mere memory dismays me, still I will tell you about it.

After my uncle departed, I devoted all my time to study (indeed this is why I had stayed behind); then I bathed, ate dinner, and had a restless and brief sleep. Earlier, for the duration of many days, the earth had shaken, but this fact did not cause fear, because earthquakes are a commonly observed phenomenon in Campania; but that night they grew so great that I would say it seemed as if everything was in upheaval, and not just moving. We stayed in the courtyard of the house, a small space that separates the houses from the beach. I don't know if I should call it courage or lack of awareness (in fact I was barely eighteen years old). I sent for a volume of Livy, and to pass the time I read and also took notes, as I had begun to do earlier. Then a friend of my uncle, recently arrived from Spain, came to check on us. Since he saw my mother and me sitting in the courtyard, and I moreover reading, he chastised her for her laziness and me for my thoughtlessness. But this did not stop me from reading.

It was already the first hour of the day, and yet the light was still faint and almost languid. The buildings around us were shaken, and since we were in an open, if narrow space, we were very frightened that a collapse was imminent. Only then did we decide to leave town. A stunned crowd followed us and, in their terror taking it for prudence, preferred our plan to those of others, and in a great mass followed on our heels and swept us along. Having left the town we stopped. There we witnessed many strange and frightful things. Even though the terrain was flat, the vehicles we had ordered prepared slipped back and could not stay in place, even with stones as supports. Moreover it seemed as if the sea were folding back on itself, almost as if pushed back by the earthquake.

Certainly the beach was broader and many sea animals were left on dry sand. From the other direction a black and terrible cloud, ripped apart by twisting flames, opened up vast flashes of fire. These were similar to lightning, but even larger.

The same friend who had come from Spain exclaimed loudly and insistently: "If your brother, your uncle, lives, he wants you to be safe; if he has perished, he would want you to survive. Why then do you hesitate to flee?" We answered that, uncertain about his fate, we didn't feel we could think of our own. He waited no further, and immediately left us and removed himself from danger at full speed. After a short time that cloud lowered toward earth and covered the sea; it enveloped and hid Capreae and hid from view the promontory of Misenum. Then my mother began to beg me, implore me, order me to try to flee in some way. I could do this because I am young, but she could not, because of her age and the heaviness of her body. She was quite content to die, but not to be the cause of my death. I disagreed; I wouldn't save myself without her. Then, taking her by the hand, I forced her to quicken her pace. She succeeded with difficulty and moaned that she was delaying me. Ash was already falling, but it still was not dense. I turned around; a dense cloud loomed behind us and, like a torrent rushing over the land, it pressed down on us. "Let us pull away from the crowd," I said, "as long as we can see, because if we fall in this darkness we will be trampled by the crowd behind us." We had just sat down when night fell, not as when there is no moon or the sky is cloudy, but as when you find yourself in a closed room with the lamps spent. You could hear the wails of women, the cries of children, the shouts of men. Some called out loud, looking for their parents, others their children, others their spouses, and they recognized each other from their voices. Some lamented their fate, others the fate of their loved ones. There were some who, fearing death, prayed for it to come. Many raised their arms to the gods, others, more numerous, declared that the gods were no longer, and that this was the last night on earth. Some magnified the real dangers with imaginary and false terrors. There were those who announced, falsely, but they were believed, that Misenum had collapsed or was in flames. A faint light reappeared, which did not seem to us like daytime, but rather the beginning of the approaching fire. But this stopped at a distance and again there was darkness, again ash in great quantity and depth. Every now and then we got up to shake the ash off our backs, otherwise we would have been covered and even squashed under its weight. I can be proud that even under such perils, I never uttered a lament or anything other than a manly expression, but I found great comfort in death, thinking that I was perishing along with everyone, and with me, sadly, the world.

Finally the cloud lifted and vanished in a sort of smoke or fog. Then it was truly day, and the sun even appeared, but livid, as when there is an eclipse. To our still frightened eyes the landscape looked changed and covered by a thick blanket of ash, as if it had snowed. After returning to Misenum and recovering our strength as best we could, we passed a troubled and uncertain night, suspended between hope and fear. The fear prevailed; since the earthquake jolts continued and many, out of their minds, made terrifying prophecies, almost mocking the evil that had befallen them and others. Even then, however, since we had escaped danger and expected new ones, we did not think about leaving, until we had received news of my uncle.

You will read these details, certainly not worthy of history, without judging them of use for your writings, and you will take the blame if they are not even worthy of a letter, for you have asked me for them. Farewell.

The Effects of the Eruption in Pompeii and Stabiae

The beginning of the paroxysmal phase of the eruption, which took place at 1:00 p.m. on August 24, A.D. 79, was noted in Cape Misenum by Gaius Pliny Secundus, the famous naturalist and commander of the Roman fleet stationed there. An enormous mushroom cloud rose from Mount Vesuvius, climbing high in the sky and spreading out, assuming a branched formation that, due to the prevailing winds, seemed to extend toward the southeast (fig. 65). The distance that separated Cape Misenum (about 30 kilometers) from Vesuvius made it impossible to perceive the signs of the initial phase of the eruption, which probably consisted of a series of small explosions in the early morning (between 9:00 and 10:00 a.m. of August 24). For this reason these events are not mentioned in Pliny's first letter. The initial activity, in fact, was characterized by a modest flow of material emitted from a low eruptive cloud, attested to by the thin layer of gray ash, rich in

65. Development of the eruptive column during the 1980 eruption of Mount St. Helens.

66. Villas on the slopes of Vesuvius (photo G. Sommer, late 1800s).

pisolitic deposits, at the base of subsequent pyroclastic layers. This was the result of a series of phreatic explosions, caused by the interaction of the surface acquifer with the upper portion of the magma. These exploded materials were then deposited along the sides of Vesuvius and in the areas east of and closest to the volcano, alarming the people who inhabited those zones (fig. 66). This ash was discovered in the Rustic Villas one and two, near present-day Terzigno. It had been deposited on the floors of the wine cellars, which were built without roofing, and in other open areas and entryways. This event corresponded to the opening of the volcanic conduit, with the progressive expulsion of the masses that had obstructed it, facilitating the rising of the magma. In a passage by Cassius Dio, who evidently transcribed sources not reported in Pliny the Younger's first letter, we probably have testimony about what happened that morning of August 24: …*a great and sudden crash was heard, as if the mountains were being knocked down, one upon the other. Then stones of immense size also began to spew out, and to touch even the highest peaks; thus a tremendous quantity of fire and smoke escaped…*(*Hist. Rom.* LXVI, 21–23).

In Cape Misenum, Pliny the Elder, goaded by his curiosity as a naturalist, decided to equip a Liburnian galley (a light boat with an elongated shape, narrowed at bow and stern, with two rows of oars), in order to observe the eruptive phenomena from a closer vantage point. While he was about to embark (around 2:30 p.m.) a messenger arrived with an urgent request for help from Rectina. This acquaintance, the wife of Caesius Bassus, lived in a villa at the foot of Vesuvius, where the effects of the volcano's first phase of activity apparently had already arrived that morning (fig. 67). The location of Rectina's villa, mentioned in the first letter, would seem to be confirmed by the estimate that it would have taken about four hours for the messenger to arrive at Cape Misenum, using a coastal road; it would have been possible to travel by sea toward Naples due to winds blowing in the opposite direction.

This passage by Pliny the Younger may be merely a literary device thought up to cloak his uncle's scientific curiosity in a courageous humanitarian gesture, one that would more befit his post as admiral. If, however, it corresponds to reality, then we would have indirect proof that the initial phase of activity took place in the early hours of the morning of the 24th, between 9:00 and 10:00. Pliny the Elder immediately changed his plans and ordered that some quadriremes be prepared, in order to rescue not only Rectina but also the greatest possible number of people who lived in the area most directly affected by the eruption. Thus his final heroic voyage began in the early hours of the afternoon of August 24, and he dictated his observations about what was happening to an unknown collaborator. We have no direct account of the situation in Pompeii, Stabiae, and the other settlements scattered throughout the region southeast of Vesuvius, but we can imagine the consternation and fear that struck those living there who, while going about their normal everyday activities, were caught unawares by a phenomenon of such vast dimensions that it blocked out the sun and was accompanied by deafening noise and continuous earthquake shocks.

Approximately 30 minutes after the beginning of the explosive phase of the eruption, an enormous cloud rose above Vesuvius to a height of about 15 kilometers. It dispersed southeast of the volcano, following the prevailing winds, and started to release a dense, continuous cascade of pyroclastic materials, made up of white pumice and, to a lesser degree, of stones, lapilli, and ash. In Pompeii, in particular, these materials began to accumulate rapidly in the streets, the green spaces, the atriums, and on the flat rooftops of buildings. The inhabitants, increasingly

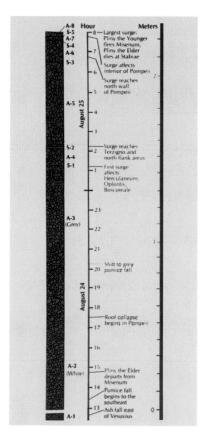

67. Timeline of the eruptive events that took place between August 24 and 27, A.D. 79, reconstructed by H. Sigurdsson in the 1980s, on the basis of stratigraphic studies and Pliny the Younger's letters. As reported in the text, subsequent studies have shown the presence of thin cinereous levels, corresponding to the passage from the white pumice to the gray pumice stage, ascribable to two early pyroclastic surges that occurred at about 8:00 p.m. on August 24, A.D. 79 (from Cioni et al., 1992).

85

68. Imaginary reconstruction of the flight of inhabitants from Pompeii during the eruption (Anonymous, late 1800s, lithograph).

frightened and surprised by these sudden manifestations, took refuge beneath porch roofs

and balconies and inside dwellings and public buildings, to find shelter from the

69. Farmers in flight protect their faces during the eruption of Pinatubo of June 22, 1991.

continuous and bothersome rain of pumice and large pyroclasts, which could wound or kill those who remained out in the open (fig. 68).

Reaction must have been similar throughout the region affected by the fallout phase, between Pompeii and Stabiae. The local people, especially those working outside, were forced to flee their farmhouses as pumice and lapilli began to cover the fields, hillsides, and streets, making it difficult for people, animals, and vehicles to move about (fig. 69). The Sarno River began to cover over with floating pumice, rendering it unnavigable. Pumice also clogged the coastal waters, where vessels anchored in the port areas of Pompeii and Stabiae could not put out to sea, also because of strong winds and a probable sudden withdrawal of the sea. Perhaps in the early afternoon, at least part of the resident population in the area where the greatest amount of pumice fell, and where the eruptive phenomena and seismic shocks continued unabated, had already made the decision to flee, probably in the direction of the region of Nuceria. If possible they would have used baggage wagons and animals, which could still proceed with relative ease along the roads, there being only a shallow cover of pumice. About four hours after the beginning of the eruption, the weight of the accumulated pumice, in pieces approximately 40–50 centimeters in size, began to collapse the flat roofs of the buildings in Pompeii. Many structures, already destabilized by seismic shocks, were rendered unfit for habitation.

Huge quantities of pyroclastic

materials were being deposited on roads, in gardens, and in the countryside, while the flight of inhabitants from crowded urban areas, villas, and farms scattered throughout the region intensified. People carried whatever valuables they were able to recover, particularly coins and jewels. They moved with difficulty through the darkness that prevailed, due to the dense eruptive cloud emitted by the volcano, which, during this phase, rose from 14 to 26 kilometers high. It was difficult to breathe, and a continuous rain of pyroclasts blocked their passage (figs. 70 a–b). It is likely that some of the fugitives who abandoned Pompeii and the immediate outskirts sought shelter in buildings used for storage at the river port along the Sarno, the current site of Murecine. Others, seeking to escape by sea and seeing that this was impossible, took shelter near the seaport, in the

70a. People fleeing Vesuvius's rain of ashes during the eruption of 1906. The scene effectively depicts what might have happened during the eruption of A.D. 79.

70b. Pompeii, Removal of the layer of pumice inside a residence (photo Esposito, late 1800s).

area of present-day Bottaro. We will never be able to reconstruct the agitation of those dramatic moments, but we will not be far from the reality if we heed a passage in the second letter of Pliny the Younger. The passage refers to the events that occurred during the night and shortly before dawn on August 25, in Cape Misenum, as does a passage by Cassius Dio:

You could hear the wails of women, the cries of children, the shouts of men. Some called out loud, looking for their parents, others their children, others their spouses, and they recognized each other from their voices. Some lamented their fate, others the fate of their loved ones.
There were some who, fearing death, prayed for it to come. Many raised their arms to the gods, others, more numerous, declared that the gods were no longer, and that this was the last night on earth. (PLINY, *Letters* VI, 20); *Others were of the opinion either that the entire world had been reduced again to chaos, or that it was to be consumed by fire; and for that reason others hurried from their houses to go out in the streets, others from the streets to take shelter in their houses; as still others went from sea to land, or from land to sea, reduced to a state of agitation…* (CASSIUS DIO, *Hist. Rom.* LXVI, 21–23).

While events developed in increasingly dramatic fashion for the local population, Pliny the Elder attempted in vain to disembark, during the course of the afternoon, at an unspecified point along the Vesuvian coast. He was unsuccessful, due to the continuous rain of pumice and ash on the ships and the sudden appearance of a shoal, *"vadum subitum,"* which made it impossible to approach the shore. The precise point where Pliny attempted to disembark has been the subject of debate. Some hypothesize that it was near Herculaneum, thinking that the shoal originated from the arrival of the first pyroclastic flows, which therefore would already have reached the city of Herculaneum and the beach area by the early afternoon. Others place the site further south, in which case it is important to keep certain considerations in mind: a) the area where he attempted to disembark was subject to a dense fall of pyroclasts, as Pliny himself recounts (VI, 16), and precisely because of what he describes in his first letter, we believe he was not writing about the area of Herculaneum, since the city was not affected by the first phase of the eruption; b) on the other hand, in his text Pliny never mentions Herculaneum, an important city in the Vesuvian area, directly overlooking the sea; c) the direction of the winds blowing from the northwest made it difficult to move quickly toward the Herculanean coast; d) the unexpected shoal, the result of the conjunction of accumulating fallen pyroclastic material and a partial withdrawal of the sea, causing a rise in the sea bottom, occurred before the eruption, as mentioned earlier in regard to the beach at Herculaneum. For this reason we feel it is safer to locate Pliny's disembarkation spot along the coast between Torre del Greco and Oplontis, if not precisely in the area of Pompeii.

At this point in his voyage, Pliny the Elder noted the impossibility of disembarking along the Vesuvian coast, which was being assaulted by a dense rain of pumice and stones. He was unable to return to Misenum, due to winds blowing in the opposite direction, and so he gave orders to move toward Stabiae (14 kilometers south of Vesuvius), a place that could more easily be reached before nightfall, and where his friend Pomponianus lived, in a villa along the coast.

The Stabian area began receiving significant downpours of pumice (fig. 71), and certainly during the afternoon the continuous rain of pyroclasts had alarmed the inhabitants. The pumice accumulations began to threaten the stability of buildings, some of which were probably already affected by partial roof collapses. The inhabitants, terrified by these sudden manifestations, were

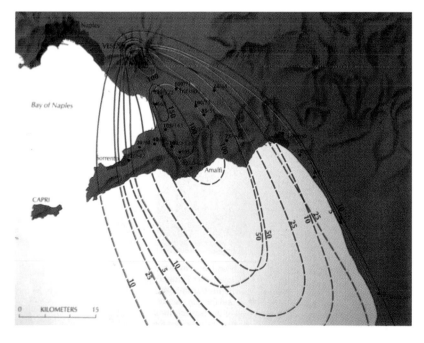

71. Area of pumice distribution during the eruption of A.D. 79 (from Sigurdsson *et al.*, 1985).

preparing to flee, but were not yet panicked. Ascertaining the impossibility of leaving by sea, some decided to remain, taking refuge in buildings that were still fit for use, while others took flight by land, in the direction of Nuceria.

Pliny the Elder, after having made his way across the last stretch of sea, thanks to favorable winds arrived at around 7:00 p.m. near the port area beneath the hill of Varano, in Stabiae. Thus he succeeded in meeting up with his friend Pomponianus, who had already readied some boats for an attempted flight. He was, however, unable to weigh anchor, due to the strong winds blowing toward the Vesuvian coast, which prevented him from going where he wanted but which had favored Pliny's voyage and landing. At the moment of his arrival, the Stabian area would have seemed affected only by a slight rain of white pumice. This would not have constituted an immediate danger, and it was not until nighttime that considerable quantities of ash and gray pumice reached Stabiae. Pomponianus therefore led his guest to his villa, probably on the hill of Varano, to wash up and dine, since by now it would have been evening.

During the first seven hours of volcanic activity, about 1.4 meters of pyroclastic material had been deposited in Pompeii, along with a huge quantity over the rest of the region to the southeast, contributing to the destabilization of residential structures, particularly in Terzigno and Oplontis. Around 8:00 p.m. an abrupt change in the chemical-physical properties of the magma created an emission of gray pumice of greater size and density. This transitional phase was also marked by two levels of pyroclastic flows (Sa, Sb) identified in the area of Terzigno and caused by the first collapses of the eruptive column. In fact, an increase in the quantity of magma emitted and a progressive decrease in the substantially volatile content in the course of eruption led to partial collapses of the eruptive column. The column became denser than the surrounding air, creating the first pyroclastic flows that affected the areas to the east closest to Vesuvius.

In Terzigno these flows caused extensive damage to buildings in the area, killing the twelve people discovered inside Villas 2 and 6. Immediately thereafter the fallout resumed. Deposits of gray pumice caused the collapse of the roofs that previously had resisted the arrival of the first flows, as we know from the numerous masonry fragments found at this level.

In the meantime, in Oplontis the accumulations of pumice caused the partial collapse of the roofs and external colonnades of Villa A, the so-called Villa of Poppaea. Numerous individuals sought shelter in the nearby complex B (figs. 72 a–b).

It was now the night between August 24 and 25. Pliny, after being refreshed, observed extensive fires on the slopes of Vesuvius, which he explained away as farms in flames, abandoned by farmers; he then went to lie down, unaware that he had witnessed the quickening of events with the formation of two more surges that reached the areas closest to the volcano between one and two in the morning.

What Pliny observed can be identified with surges S1 and S2, which, with notable velocity, struck Herculaneum, the site of Oplontis, the area of Boscoreale, and once again Terzigno, completing its destruction with the burying of all settlements in the area and instantaneously extinguishing all signs of life.

Surge S1, which originated around one in the morning, extended along the south and west sides of the volcano, overwhelming in particular the farm known as Villa Regina, in Boscoreale, and the buildings in Oplontis. It was probably this event that caused the death of the 54 individuals who sought refuge in a space on the ground floor of Villa B, known as the villa of Lucius Crassius Tertius (fig. 73), and next to

72a–b. Oplontis, Villa A. The columns of the portico, knocked down during the pumice downpour phase.

73. Oplontis, Villa B. Discovery of human bodies.

91

74a. Pompeii, House of Successus. Table support in the shape of a small statue of a child, discovered, still covered by pumice, in the peristyle.

which a considerable quantity of jewels and gold and silver coins were found. Surge S2, around two in the morning, devastated the entire north side of Vesuvius, destroying the rustic villas near Terzigno. At the same time, in Pompeii and the rest of the region to the southeast, the fall of pyroclasts continued throughout the entire night until dawn. During this phase the eruptive column reached the frightening height of 32 kilometers. In the ancient city the level of pumice increased by about another 1.2 meters, reaching on average 2.6–2.8 meters, from the time the eruption began (2–2.5 meters in Stabiae). The accumulation of pyroclastic materials rose up from the street level until it reached the upper stories of houses, easily penetrating doors, windows, roofs, and floors, demolishing buildings and piling up in atriums, peristyles, and gardens (figs. 74 a–b).

Many people who did not escape from the city between the afternoon and night of the 24th took shelter in the ground-floor spaces of buildings and were trapped by the accumulations of pumice that blocked doors and windows. They died from progressive asphyxiation, or during a late attempt at flight. Other victims of the fallout phase died from collapsing roofs, as attested to by discoveries of skeletons covered with masonry materials (fig. 75). At the same time, some groups had sought refuge in indoor spaces that the pumice had not reached (ground floors, lower floors, and basements), where they still were able to flee. Still others fled to the upper floors of buildings, since the pumice had invaded the floors below and blocked every escape route. During the night and until just before dawn, strong earthquakes shook the entire Vesuvian area, from Misenum to Stabiae. The sea was observed to have pulled back, a phenomenon connected to the beginning of an intense phreatomagmatic phase. This was caused by the collapse of the roof of the magmatic chamber, following its partial emptying during the violent Plinian phase, and the entry of acquifer fluids deep within the magmatic system. Large internal explosions followed, causing the volcanic edifice and

74b. Pompeii, large Palaestra, excavation of the north portico, with the eruptive layers clearly evident.

75. Pompeii, House of Trebius Valens. Four bodies discovered in the pumice-covered peristyle.

the surrounding area to swell. On the morning of the 25th the fall of pumice became less intense. The surviving Pompeians, having taken refuge earlier inside the city's houses, put their faith in this period of apparent calm and went out in search of an escape route from the city. These fugitives headed toward the southern sector of the city, to reach the roads leading out. They often walked in small groups, making their way uneasily due to the pumice deposits and breathing with difficulty because of the ash-filled air. They carried lanterns to help with the poor visibility. In Stabiae, after Pliny lay down to rest, there was an incessant fall of gray pumice that lasted the rest of the night. As dawn grew near on the 25th, Pomponianus woke Pliny in the space where he was sleeping. The door almost could not be opened, due to the accumulation of pumice in the open space outside the room, perhaps an atrium or a peristyle. The earthquake shocks also intensified, and Pliny, Pomponianus, and their companions, after tying pillows to their heads, abandoned the villa, deciding that it was better to risk being struck by the rain of pumice than by a collapse of the villa's walls (fig. 76). During this phase the residents in the Stabian area who still remained came to a similar decision. They abandoned their shelters and went in search of an escape route.

Dawn was now near, but darkness continued to reign, due to the dense clouds of ash that, spewing forth from Vesuvius, were pushed toward the southeast by the winds. In Pompeii it became difficult to breathe or see:

It was already daytime, but nighttime reigned, darker and deeper than any other (*Letters* VI, 16). Around 6:30 an increase in activity created a new surge (S3), the first to reach Pompeii. The cloud stopped along the north side of the city wall, unable to move beyond it. It caused the deaths by suffocation of those who had taken shelter in the underground spaces of the Villa of the Mysteries and the Villa of Diomedes, outside the Herculaneum Gate, and the individuals travelling along the Via delle Tombe. Suddenly the volcanic edifice shook with tremendous rumbling, and beginning around 7:30 produced three surges that, in half an hour, overran and buried Pompeii. The first two surges (S4 and S5), a few minutes apart, poured over the city walls and reached the inner areas of the city. It took Pompeians wandering the streets completely by surprise; they were overwhelmed and suffocated by the gases and inhaled ash (fig. 77). The same fate awaited those who still had not fled their

76. Stabiae, Villa San Marco.

77. Imaginary reconstruction of the flight of the inhabitants during the eruption (Anonymous, late 1800s, lithograph).

95

78. Pompeii, House of Julius Polibius. Human body discovered in the layer of ash on the surface level in an interior room of the house.

houses, hoping that the eruptive fury of the volcano would abate, as well as those who had taken shelter on the upper floors of buildings or in interior or basement level spaces, or on the lower floors (fig. 78). They probably thought these areas would provide good shelter, since they were safe from the dense rain of ash and pumice (fig. 79). Most of the victims of these two pyroclastic surges, both indoors and out, were discovered between layers of ash about 15–20 centimeters thick, deposited by the two surges (fig. 80). Continuing their deadly and destructive course, the surges took only a few minutes to

79. Schematic reconstruction of ways victims were buried during the various phases of the eruption (from R.W. Nicholson, National Geographic Artist, 120, 5, 1961).

strike the entire region south of Pompeii, arriving at the seaport near the coastal lagoon and the river port on the Sarno. They killed all those who were still hoping to escape the eruption's fury.

In these two locations especially, large groups of victims were discovered during excavations carried out between the late 1800s and the early 1900s. In the first area eighty-eight bodies were discovered, some seventy-eight in the ash inside shops and taverns located along a road. These may have been people who were fleeing from neighboring areas, expecting a diminution of eruptive activity and hoping to escape by sea. In the second area forty-six bodies were found, ten in the pumice, perhaps people who lived on the outskirts of the city. The remaining bodies were discovered in a layer of ash, leading to the supposition that these individuals came from Pompeii proper by road, near the Stabian Gate, in an attempt to flee by river, but had died when they were overtaken by the surges.

In Oplontis, surge S5 left a deposit more than 1 meter thick, cutting off much of the top of the walls of Villa A. Later, at the end of the eruption, pyroclastic waves brought in the full depth of volcanic materials, about 5 meters, completely burying the cluster of buildings.

Around eight in the morning an enormous pyroclastic cloud was emitted (S6), bringing the most destructive of the surges that violently struck the city of Pompeii. This caused the collapse of the highest building walls, and, in the violence of its crush, carried along a great variety of building materials and in some cases the bodies of victims. This was the most

80. Pompeii, House of the Cryptoportico. The discovery of a group of fugitives in the building's garden.

81. An inexorably advancing surge, which originated during the eruption of Pinatubo in June 1991, threatens people who are fleeing in a jeep.

surge continued its violent and destructive course over the rest of the region, reaching Stabiae and forcing the remaining inhabitants to flee in disarray; here too there were victims. Earlier, Pliny the Elder, after leaving the house of Pomponianus, went to the beach below the hill of Varano, attempting to flee by sea with his retinue. Seeing that this was impossible due to the rough waters and the steady winds working against them, he stayed there, awaiting a more propitious moment. The cloud, preceded by lightning and fire and by a strong smell of sulfur in the air, reached the beach, causing the death of Pliny by suffocation (fig. 82). It is likely that part of his retinue managed to flee to safety at the last moment, finding shelter nearby.

The terrifying cloud extended over the entire region and the Vesuvian coast, also reaching the Bay of Naples. It pushed as

destructive event of all in Pompeii, which was by now buried beneath a blanket of pyroclastic deposits about 1.20 meters deep (fig. 81). The same

82. Stabiae, death of Pliny the Elder on the beach (Pierre-Henri de Valenciennes, 1813, oil on canvas).

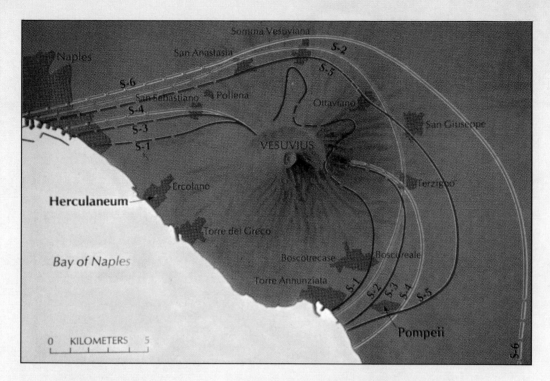

far as Misenum, where it forced Pliny the Younger to flee with his mother and the other inhabitants of the city (fig. 83).

THE EFFECTS OF THE ERUPTION IN HERCULANEUM

The city of Herculaneum, located only seven miles west of the crater of Vesuvius, was buried beneath a blanket of pyroclastic materials more than twenty meters deep. Because of the wind direction during the Plinian phase of the fall, the city was only marginally affected by the rain of pumice that had so violently assailed Pompeii and the region southeast of the volcano. In fact, in Herculaneum the reconstruction of the progress of the volcanic deposits has made it possible to ascertain that the first phase of volcanic activity deposited only a few

centimeters of pumice material. Excavations in the area of the city and the nearby Villa of the Papyri have revealed that the series of pyroclastic flows and surges, which characterized the second phase of the eruption, buried the city, attacking at a speed of at least 100 kilometers per hour. This caused the destruction of masonry structures and the death of all but those who had managed to leave the city earlier. Certainly the residents of Herculaneum noticed the first manifestations of the reawakening of volcanic activity, on the morning of August 24, as did everyone who lived near the slopes of Vesuvius. The formation of a first eruptive cloud alarmed and worried the inhabitants, who did not understand what was happening to the familiar

83. Area of distribution of deposits left by surges during the eruption (from Sigurdsson *et al.*, 1985).

84. Herculaneum. Imaginary reconstruction of the final moments of life of the inhabitants of the city (Anonymous, late 1800s, lithograph).

mountain whose mass loomed over the city. Their fears increased after the beginning of the paroxysmal phase, around 1:00 p.m., with the formation of an enormous mushroom cloud, noted by Pliny the Elder. During the early afternoon, the inhabitants remained undecided about what to do. Then, due to the terrifying appearance of the cloud, now so vast it obscured the sun, the roar that accompanied the eruption, and the continuous earthquake shocks, the people of Herculaneum fled, rather than take shelter inside the buildings, with the exception of a few houses. They used the coastal road that passed upstream, near the city in the direction of Naples, or they tried to set out in boats in the port area.

People behaved completely differently, but understandably, compared to the population residing in the area southeast of the Vesuvian region. There the continuous fall of pyroclasts made it difficult to flee by foot, and for some hours it had been impossible to escape with the help of vehicles or animals, so some were convinced to take shelter in buildings. The people of Herculaneum who lingered in that city did not have time to grasp what was happening when they were surprised by the first lethal surge, about one in the morning of August 25. This was caused by a first, partial collapse of the eruptive cloud, which, rolling along the sides of the volcano, reached Herculaneum within a matter of minutes, killing the few inhabitants who had remained in their houses. (In fact, thirty-two bodies were discovered in the excavated area of the city, eight in the House of Primigenius Granianus.) After a few seconds the surge broke over the beach, penetrating within the barrel vaults where numerous people had taken refuge, killing them instantaneously, and finally coming to the end of its course after moving out into the sea for some scores of meters (fig. 84). According to the current state of research, 296 victims were discovered, some 237 of whom were inside the barrel vaults beneath the Suburban Quarter. This probably indicates that part of the population chose this extreme and unlucky refuge, hoping that when the eruptive fury came to an end, they would be able to escape the city by sea (fig. 85). The presence of both young children and the elderly among the victims might signify that these people's flight did not occur precipitously. Indeed, it is possible that their descent from the city toward beachside sanctuaries they considered safe took place with relative calm, at an unspecified time, but prior to the arrival of the surges. The first surge (S1) bore down on the city in turbulent fashion, with a temperature of about 400° C (752° F). It moved at low velocity due to the obstruction created by the buildings, and thus for the most part did not carry off or crush the structures, objects, or even the people. Their bodies were discovered in the positions they assumed as they died, with

85. Herculaneum. The Suburban Quarter, with bath facilities and barrel vaults overlooking the sea.

101

86. Herculaneum, human bodies discovered inside a barrel vault on the shoreline.

87. Herculaneum, barrel vault seven, skeleton number five.

88. Herculaneum, beach. Female body number sixty-five with gold jewelry, discovered in 1983 outside barrel vault nine.

their skeletons practically whole (figs. 86–87).

Near the bodies, numerous finds were discovered, both precious, such as gold jewelry (fig. 88), coins, and silver plate, and commonplace, such as the ever-present house keys in iron and bronze, bronze coins, small glass containers, perhaps for perfumes, and oil lamps, the latter an indication of the darkness that blanketed the city. Unusual objects also were found, such as a box with surgical instruments and a short sword and dagger along with a holster belt, indicating the presence of a doctor and a soldier among the victims. Recent studies carried out on the bony remains have shown that the people of Herculaneum did not die from asphyxiation, as in Pompeii, but due to rapid exposure to the intense heat that developed from the cloud. Those who remained on the beach were subjected to the full effects of the surge, and, upon contact with the incandescent material borne by the cloud, were thrown to the ground and died instantaneously from the immediate boiling and vaporization of their organic liquids and tissues. Those who had found shelter within the barrel vaults did not feel the direct action of the surge, but died from the shock of their burns, due to the elevated temperature of the cloud. This is why in Herculaneum the layer of ash did not reveal cavities corresponding to the bodies of victims, a situation that in Pompeii made it possible to reconstruct figures by pouring plaster into spaces that had been left by the progressive disintegration of human tissue around the skeletons.

The first surge, which left a deposit in the city of about 40–50

centimeters, and about 150 centimeters in the barrel vaults along the shore, was followed by a pyroclastic flow, F1, characterized by a higher concentration of solid particles and derived from the same eruptive cloud. The flow worked its way into preexisting depressions in the land, distributing itself around the promontory of Herculaneum. It assaulted only the southern quarter of the city, characterized by the important palaestra building. It then reached the beach, where it surrounded a large boat that was discovered overturned near the Suburban Baths, and then went on for about 40 meters into the sea, leaving a deposit of only a few centimeters. The next surge, S2, around two in the morning, was less hot but quicker (around 30 meters per second). It caused extensive damage to the masonry structures of buildings, leaving a deposit of about 1.5 meters of pyroclastic material. It carried along a considerable amount of building materials, including bricks, parts of walls, and pieces of carbonized wood (figs. 89 a–d).

Surge S2 was associated with a second flow (F2). Like the first

89a. Herculaneum. Lararium shaped like a temple, in carbonized wood.

89b. Herculaneum. House of the Wood Sacellum, temple-shaped lararium, in carbonized wood.

89c. Herculaneum. House of the Bicentenary, wing number seven, double-door sliding gate that folds back up to the ceiling, in carbonized wood.

89d. Herculaneum. House of the Carbonized Furniture, space number eight, day bed in carbonized wood.

flow, it ran along the sides of the city, as we know by the presence of thinner deposits toward the center of the city. On the beach it left about 5 meters of pyroclastic materials, consolidated in appearance and rich in pumice, which completely filled the barrel vaults.

The third surge (S3, 10 centimeters deep) and its related flow (F3, approximately 10 meters deep) finally covered what remained of Herculaneum, leaving only the top of the Theater exposed. At dawn, subsequent pyroclastic flows (S and F 4, 5, 6) overflowed into an area previously buried by the first clouds, forming a layer of volcanic material 23 meters deep in all and destroying more lives and property in Pompeii. Materials transported by these pyroclastic flows piled up along the beach and sea below Herculaneum creating a new coastline that extended out some 400 meters from the old one (figs. 90–91). A recent study of the positioning of furnishings at the moment of their discovery in the buildings of Herculaneum, based on the Excavation Journals related particularly to the period of 1927–1940, provides new data that quantifies the distribution of the flows that assailed the city. Pyroclastic flows subsequent to the first one ran through the streets with ease, especially through the cardines, which sloped toward the sea. These flows caused various types of damage to the masonry structures facing directly onto the streets, depending on the building materials' degree of resistance. Moreover the flows penetrated buildings, creating the greatest damage in the areas closest to the streets, while the interior spaces

91. Herculaneum. Current coastline, with the excavated area of the city, the modern city, and Vesuvius in the background.

remained better preserved. Evidence has shown that the initial flows were more fluid in nature and moved both laterally and vertically, according to analysis of the Excavation Journals. These analyses locate the precise positioning, in relationship to both the walls and floor levels of rooms, for almost all the finds discovered inside the city. In fact, numerous objects were found to have been pushed toward the walls of rooms, or upward to the height of the top floor. In other cases, however, probably in areas off to the sides where the flow lost its disruptive force, furnishings remained in situ, encompassed within the pyroclastic materials of the deposit. As for the structures of buildings, the impact of the flows differed, depending on both the altitude of the areas struck and the degree of resistance of the masonry. In particular, the extensive state of destruction of houses located on the edge of the promontory and

90. Eruption of the La Soufrière volcano (island of Montserrat); the overflow of pyroclastic clouds in the sea created a delta.

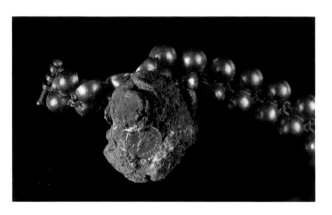

92. Herculaneum, barrel vault eight. Gold bracelet with lump of embedded silver and gold coins, discovered in 1992 between skeletons eleven and twelve.

93-94. View of the landscape surrounding Mount St. Helens after the catastrophic eruption of May 1980.

the Suburban Quarter below is tied to the increasingly strong acceleration of the flow of pyroclastics, due to the slope of the land and the different levels of the city. This material was mixed with a wide variety of detritus coming from buildings uphill in the city and from surrounding areas, as seen from the number of tree trunks found along the coastal area.

Finally, with regard to the temperature of the clouds that descended on the city, the study of metal finds discovered in the layer deposited by the first surge (S1), close to the victims along the shore, has shown gold coins and jewels in an optimum state of preservation. Bronze and silver coins were fused together, as were five silver vases in barrel vault eight. The fusion temperature of gold is a bit over 1000° C (1832° F), while for silver it is around 900° C (1652° F). By contrast, most of the bronze objects and coins discovered within subsequent pyroclastic deposits, in the houses of Herculaneum, were in an excellent state of preservation. These data allow us to conclude that the materials in silver and bronze, discovered in the shoreline area

in the first surge deposit, were partially fused and "corroded" following exposure to high temperature. But the temperature was lower than the 700–800° C (1292–1472° F) stage at which these metals begin to lose their consistency, and there must have been chemical agents, transported by the cloud, that attacked the objects' surfaces (fig. 92). According to recent studies carried out on the skeletons, these archaeological data confirm that the first cloud had a higher temperature than subsequent waves, which are estimated to have been about 400° C (752° F). However we cannot exclude the possibility that higher temperatures peaked for brief periods within the cloud that acted upon the finds.

THE FINAL PHASE OF THE ERUPTION

The final phase of the eruption was still characterized by phreatomagmatic activity, caused by the interaction of magma and surface water, with the formation of at least three more large flows. The first two were confined to the areas closest to Vesuvius, and the third corresponded to the second cloud of ash described by Pliny the Younger, which reached as far as Misenum. The activity of Vesuvius continued for days with lesser violence. In the end the tops of the highest walls were the only things left unburied, the sole testimony that remained of the city of Pompeii. Herculaneum had completely disappeared, and the entire region had taken on the appearance of a desert. The morphology of the

volcano was transformed radically: the terrible eruption had destroyed its summit, and the mountain took on the desolate appearance described by Statius and Martial about ten years after the catastrophe. They wrote of ash that, like a mournful blanket, covered the landscape that had until then been green and lush: *Such songs I intoned for you, Marcellus, from the Cumaean shores where Vesuvius vented its convulsive wrath, pouring out fires that rivaled the flames of Aetna. Surprising faith! When the crops are reborn and these deserts flower anew, will a fortune-seeking generation of men believe that beneath their feet lie cities and people, and that their ancestral companions were swallowed up below? And yet this summit does not cease its mortal threat (Silvae, IV, 4, 78–86); Here is Vesuvius, so recently verdant with shaded vines, here prized grapes overflowed the vats; Bacchus loved these slopes more than the hills of Nysa, in the past satyrs performed their dance on this mountain; this was Venus's abode, more agreeable to her than Sparta, this was the place named for Hercules. Now all lies submerged in flames and in sad stone; now the gods must regret that it was they who allowed such power to be exercised here (Epigram IV, 44)* (figs. 93–94). After the catastrophe, the emperor Titus sent a commission to the sites struck hardest by the event, the *guardians restoring Campania*. They were charged with beginning to rebuild the destroyed cities, utilizing the assets of those who died during the eruption of Vesuvius without heirs: *he drew at random among former consuls for those who would be responsible for the rebuilding of Campania and for the rebuilding of the destroyed cities, he set aside the assets of those who had died during the eruption of Vesuvius without leaving heirs (De vita Caesarum, Titus, 8, 3-4).*

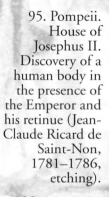

95. Pompeii. House of Josephus II. Discovery of a human body in the presence of the Emperor and his retinue (Jean-Claude Ricard de Saint-Non, 1781–1786, etching).

The Discovery
of Human Bodies in Pompeii

In Herculaneum, human bodies (a total of 338 verified victims) were, except in rare cases, discovered during recent excavations and were immediately studied, as they also were in Oplontis and Terzigno. In Pompeii, however, the discovery of victims is intertwined with the adventurous and troubled history of the early years of the city's rediscovery. The first indication of a discovery of a human body dates back to April 19, 1748, about two months after explorations in the area of Pompeii began. When buildings were excavated at the intersection of the Via Stabia and the Via Nola, a victim of the eruption was discovered with a hoard of coins, in the layer of ash deposited by the surge above the pumice.

In the decades that followed, as the portion of the city that was uncovered continued to grow, the number of human bodies found also increased, arousing the interest of treasure seekers (fig. 95), due to the frequent presence of coins, gems, gold jewelry, and silver plate. The victims had taken these valuables from their homes, often in small wooden boxes or wrapped in cloth.

The importance ascribed to these finds depended on their monetary value, or in some cases on the unusual nature of the objects, such as surgical instruments or weapons, and their scientific significance was ignored. The bodies unleashed sentimental and emotional feelings in their discoverers, and they acquired a fantastic dimension, generating "Pompeian legends" that became popular in literature beginning in the late eighteenth century. Like innumerable other small-scale finds from Pompeii, human bones did not escape the sad fate of being transformed into "souvenirs" of visits to the excavations, deferring to a fashion that began with the earliest visits by the public to the archaeological area, and which continues unabated.

We have two interesting pieces of testimony to the singular role played by the human bones, in this case the bodies discovered in the Villa of Diomedes. Accounts of visits to Pompeii by Francois de Paule Latapie in 1776 and Hester Lynch Piozzi in 1786 relate: *...certain people want to take away the parts, something that I too have done, in order to have in my small museum a bone that is more than 17 centuries old; ...I was observing a French gentleman when I saw him put a human bone in his pocket.*

In the first half of the nineteenth century, questions began to be posed about the preservation and study of these human bones, although the approach was subtle compared to literary fantasies about their discovery. One important event occurred in 1848, when Ferdinand II, under pressure by the constitutional government established as a result of a liberal uprising, was forced to establish the Commission for the Reform of the Royal Bourbon Museum and the Excavations of Antiquities of the Kingdom. Giuseppe Fiorelli and Michele Ruggiero, prominent figures in the cultural world of the time, were named secretaries. The Commission specifically entrusted the brilliant lawyer Raffaele d'Ambra with the task of investigating the administration of the archaeological area of Pompeii, which had fallen into a serious state of disarray and neglect.

In the final report, read before the Commission on October 16, 1848, d'Ambra pointed out that, among other things, bones that were discovered, along with other types of materials, had been abandoned in the deposits without any care for suitable preservation. He moreover revealed the regrettable and unjustified refusal by the Office of Excavations to allow French chemist Jean Pierre Joseph d'Arcet to study the bones: *Perhaps they thought that this illustrious Assembly of Scholars would want to carry out some experiments in Alchemy or Natural Magic.* On the basis of the report, the Commission put together eleven proposals to reopen and protect the archaeological area of Pompeii, including the bones, which thus for the first time regained their scientific dignity: *4. To open a gallery of Pompeian skeletons, donating skulls and other skeletons to our Royal University of Studies.* However, the eleven proposals remained on paper only and could not be put into practice, due to subsequent tragic events that led to the restoration of the monarchy and the end of the brief but productive liberal period.

The problem of studying and preserving the bones was addressed once again, in 1853, due to the interest of Stefano delle Chiaje. Numerous Pompeian bones were organized in the Anatomical Museum of the Royal University of Naples, with the approval of Giulio Minervine: *We are delighted that we will be the first to have the most interesting collection of skeletal antiquities.*

Chiaje, having available such a significant number of finds, carried out the first organized study, concentrating his attention above all on the bones' anatomical-pathological aspects. Subsequently, in 1882, an important study by Giustiniano Nicolucci, founder of the Institute of Anthropology of the University of Naples, was published. He analyzed one hundred skulls from Pompeii and carried out anthropological research, in the modern understanding of the term, with the goal of establishing interconnections among the various ethnic groups present in the Pompeian population of A.D. 79.

During the nineteenth century, while the first scientific research on the skeletal finds emerged and questions were raised about their adequate preservation, some of the most significant literary works were being produced about the dramatic end of the Pompeians and the discovery of their bodies. The complex and fascinating novels of Edward George Bulwer-Lytton and Candido Augusto Vecchi are crucial in this regard. Published respectively in 1835 and 1868, using reports of the excavations and descriptions of the city as well as specific discoveries of furnishings and human bodies, they developed fantastic stories about their characters in the final moments of the city's life before the catastrophic eruption. An essay by Charles-Ernest Beulè, published in 1872, stands out among the rest. Precise information about the discoveries, including their relationship to the eruptive stratigraphy, is combined with the emotional and imaginary aspects of the discovery of bodies. An isolated voice among his contemporaries, Beulè stressed that the excavation reports, particularly from the early decades of Pompeii's rediscovery, presented the data about the discovery of skeletons in too laconic a fashion, providing very little material for scholars. But he also predicted greater accuracy in future reports and mentioned his confidence in Giuseppe Fiorelli, a leading scholar and an innovator in techniques of archaeological research, who had recently been appointed Director of Excavations.

Indeed, Fiorelli brought important changes to the history of the skeletal finds.

Appropriating a method that was already being used for furnishings and wood elements, he thought that casts could be made from bodies discovered in the beds of eruptive ash. He determined that liquid plaster could be poured into these veritable molds, and that as the casts hardened, they would keep their shape, bringing to light images of the Pompeians in their final moments of life.

The method was applied for the first time on February 5, 1863, along the Vicolo degli Scheletri, resulting in four casts of bodies identified as a family group fleeing the city (figs. 96–98). The discovery, as we can well imagine, created an incredible sensation at the time. Indeed it was amply recorded in Italian and foreign documents on Pompeii in the second half of the nineteenth century.

Over the years, the vast scientific output about Pompeii followed the progress of research. Debate continued regarding the number of inhabitants in the city, with the estimated number generally ranging between 6,400 and 20,000. But there was also discussion about the need to quantify the number of human bodies found in the city, estimated, with some variation, at about two thousand. However after Nicolucci's essay, the study of skeletal finds did not arouse any new interest until recently. Based on a study we carried out on all the Excavation Journals published since 1748, it now is possible to quantify and position all the bodies discovered within the city, as well as obtain important data for reconstructing the behavior of the Pompeians during the various eruptive phases.

In the first phase of the eruption, characterized by semi-continuous fallout activity, almost all the victims (345) were found inside buildings, with a limited number of bodies (49) discovered outside.

111

discovered in open spaces, or along the roads (319), or inside buildings (334) increased considerably.

In all, 1,047 bodies have been discovered, including the last three, found in February 2002, outside the Stabian Gate. To this total (394 of which were discovered in pumice, 653 in ash), we must add a considerable group of victims, estimated to be about 100. The information reported in the Excavation Journals does not allow us to make a precise count of this group, but their inclusion brings the total number of victims discovered to date in the area of the ancient city to about 1,150.

96. Pompeii. Cast of bodies discovered along the Vicolo degli Scheletri in 1863 (photo G. Sommer, late 1800s).

During the second phase of the eruption, the number of bodies

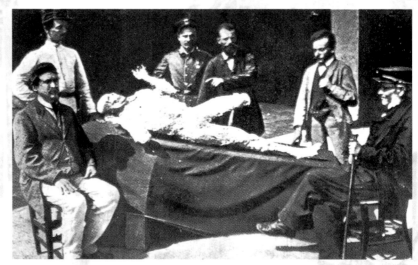

97. Pompeii. Cast of human body discovered in 1868 (photo late 1800s).

98. Pompeii. Cast of human body (photo G. Sommer, late 1800s).

Pompeian Stories and Legends

The Herculaneum Gate Sentry

The discovery, presumably in 1763, of a body in a rectangular niche on the left exterior side of the Herculaneum Gate, set the stage for a fantastic but widely believed story that began circulating in the nineteenth century about a sentry guard at one of the entrances to the city (fig. 99).

Thus the transformation of a tomb, where a victim of the eruption took shelter, into a sentry box led to the creation of the legend of the soldier. According to this legend, the soldier, faithful to his duty until the end, would not abandon his post. Holding his weapons, he allowed himself to be buried alive by the continuous rain of pumice, while the inhabitants of the city fled, terrified by the eruption hard on their heels. The description of this episode, reported by Mark Twain during a visit to Pompeii as a journalist in 1867, is unforgettable:

But perhaps the most poetical thing Pompeii has yielded to modern research, was that grand figure of a Roman soldier, clad in complete armor; who, true to his duty, true to

99. Pompeii. Herculaneum Gate, with the so-called sentry-box to the right (D. Cuciniello-L., L., R. Bianchi, 1824–1834, lithograph).

100a. Pompeii, Four-sided Portico of the Theaters (Anonymous, late 1800s, watercolor sketch).

his proud name of a soldier of Rome, and full of the stern courage which had given to that name its glory, stood to his post by the city gate, erect and unflinching, till the hell that raged around him burned out the dauntless spirit it could not conquer.[3]

THE LADY OF THE JEWELS

In the area of the Four-sided Portico of the Theaters, used by gladiators as their headquarters during the city's final period, numerous discoveries were made during the eighteenth century

100b. Pompeii, Four-sided Portico of the Theaters (photo Esposito, late 1800s).

[3] Mark Twain, *Innocents Abroad*, Chapter 31.

that allowed those writing about the city and the discoveries there to exercise their imaginations to the fullest (fig. 100). On January 9, 1768, the floor of one space yielded eighteen bodies, along with numerous gladiatorial weapons. One of the bodies was covered with precious jewelry and identified as a rich Pompeian noblewoman.

Clearly there was an inescapable element of scandal to this discovery. This unlucky woman, who took shelter with her most precious possessions as she attempted to flee, was transformed into one of those wealthy noblewomen of loose morals who vied for the favors of the heroes of the Arena. Unfortunately she chose precisely that unlucky day to pay a visit to her good-looking lover, for a secret amorous rendezvous. To complete this sad story of love and death, another body, discovered near a horse in the immediate vicinity, was identified as the servant who was entrusted with the task of accompanying the wealthy matron and protecting her from wrongdoers.

POMPEIAN DOGS

On August 30, 1787, the bodies of a man and a dog were discovered in a room in the House of the Vestals. The man's bones showed clear signs of bites. Thus it was imagined that after having died from starvation, unable to escape the room because of the continuous fall of pumice, the man was slowly devoured by his faithful friend, who had been driven mad by fear and hunger.

In the House of Vesonius Primus, however, the owners

fleeing the impending disaster left a dog tied to a chain, guarding the house, apparently with the hope of returning as soon as possible. The dog managed to remain alive during the entire period of the falling pumice, climbing up continuously on the ash accumulating in the atrium, but at dawn on August 25, the surge overwhelmed it. In 1874 a cast was made of this dog's body during the excavation of the house (fig. 101).

THE PRIESTS OF THE TEMPLE OF ISIS

The legend of the priests of Isis dates to 1813, but it is based on the 1776 discovery of two victims inside the Temple, and another in the immediate vicinity, with numerous gold and silver furnishings. According to the story, the eruption struck the priests while they were eating

101. Pompeii, House of Orpheus. Cast of dog discovered in the atrium (photo G. Sommer, late 1800s).

102a. Pompeii, Temple of Isis at the time of its discovery (P. Fabris, 1779, etching with watercolor). a meal in the large room behind the Temple, sitting around a table laid with bread, fish, and eggs. Frightened by the terrifying events, they, like many other Pompeians, were waiting for the right moment to take flight. When the rain of pumice abated, after having collected their most sacred and precious objects (gold coins, statuettes of Isis, silver plates, vases, and some cups) in a sack, some of the priests quickly ran from the Temple

102b. Pompeii, Temple of Isis. Imaginary reconstruction (Jean-Claude Ricard de Saint-Non, etching, 1781–1786).

116

(figs. 102 a–b). Within moments of leaving, the priest entrusted with carrying the sack fell because of the difficulty of moving over the pumice, spilling the contents of his precious bundle. After being helped up by his companions, they continued to flee together toward the Triangular Forum.

At that point a strong earthquake jolt brought down part of the colonnade, knocking them down, while the precious objects they were carrying scattered on the ground. Meanwhile the other priests inside the Temple were soon trapped by the continuous fall of pumice and ash. Some died from asphyxiation near a staircase behind the kitchen. One of them, the best-looking, used an axe to partially open up a path, hacking his way through some partitions in an attempt to escape, but he was blocked by a more solid wall and died from asphyxiation.

THE MATRON OF THE HOUSE OF THE FAUN

House of the Faun is one of the most important residences in Pompeii that was brought to light in 1831. In the atrium, a significant group of jewels and a skeleton were found. This discovery inspired the story of a greedy homeowner who delayed her flight, wanting to gather up her most precious possessions, whatever the risk (fig. 103). After collecting jewelry and gold coins in a bag, she attempted to flee her house, but upon reaching the entrance she was terrified by the eruption and, despairing of

being able to save herself, turned back, spilling her possessions on the floor. Taking shelter in the tablinum, she died when the roof collapsed. Contemporary accounts of the excavation relate that her body was discovered positioned in the futile act of holding up the falling ceiling with her arms.

THE VICTIMS OF THE HOUSE OF MENANDER

In the House of Menander, as in so many houses in Pompeii, some of the inhabitants were discovered during the excavations of 1931–1932. In this case, the master of the

103. Pompeii, House of the Faun. Entrance with atrium and the tablinum in the background (Th. Duclère, late nineteenth century, color lithograph).

117

they sought an escape route across the rooftops, using a bronze lamp to illuminate the darkness that enveloped the city. More courageous but equally unfortunate were two women and a little girl who had managed to reach the upper floor where they were hoping to pass through a window and flee along the street. There they were overwhelmed by the surge. However not all died attempting to abandon the house. In fact, in the slave quarters the body of the house overseer was discovered, stretched out on a bed with the skeleton of a young woman, perhaps his daughter, at his feet. While everyone fled, this man, faithful to his duty, decided to stay on, guarding the house, trusting in the will of the gods.

GROUPS IN FLIGHT

Among the innumerable victims there are many examples of family groups, or impromptu groupings of people who gave each other courage as they attempted to flee the city, walking with difficulty upon the dense layer of pumice lighting their path through the night with lanterns, when they were struck by the first surge that attacked Pompeii (fig. 105).

In 1812, along the Via delle Tombe, near the Villa of Diomedes, the body of a young bejeweled woman was found, hugging her small child to her chest, with another two children nearby. Perhaps they came from one of the many villas on the outskirts of Pompeii.

In 1820 the bodies of four women were found, with jewelry and coins nearby, along the Via Consolare, near the House of Sallustius; the group was

104. Pompeii, House of Menander, bodies discovered in room number twenty in 1931.

105. Pompeii, Regio I, Insula 22. Casts of a group of fleeing people, discovered in 1989.

house and his slaves shared the same tragic destiny (fig. 104). A first group of three bodies was found inside a room on the ground floor, armed with a pickaxe and a hoe in a desperate attempt to make an opening through the mass of pumice that had invaded the house. Another ten victims were discovered near a staircase that led to the upper floor. They had been caught as

identified as the mistress of the house, accompanied by three slaves. Delaying her departure to recover her fortune, this wealthy woman was killed as she fled the surge.

Many of those who were fleeing (approximately one hundred), coming perhaps from the southern area of the city, were found in 1937–1938, in the area of the palaestra near the amphitheater. In desperation, they had been seeking shelter beneath the portico or were attempting to flee from the city toward the road that linked Pompeii to Nuceria (fig. 106). One group found refuge inside the latrine of the palaestra, where they barricaded themselves, heedless of the desperate cries of those who remained outside beating futilely upon the door. One of the victims has been identified as a doctor, who was discovered close to the impression of a small case containing surgical instruments. Another was an athlete, of whom a cast was made; he had nearby a container of oil, which he applied to his body before competitions, and two strigils, used to wash away sweat and stroke his muscles.

The famous group of thirteen bodies from the Garden of the Fugitives was discovered in 1961. A cast was made of the group, which consisted of at least three families struck as they attempted to walk toward the Nucerian Gate. Some of the figures are recognizable, including a slave carrying a sack on his shoulders, perhaps containing food; two children holding hands who covered their heads with a pan; and a woman who had fallen to her knees, pressing a piece of fabric to her mouth in a vain

106. Pompeii, large Palaestra, north portico walls, torn down by the fury of the eruption; approximately eighty bodies, isolated or in groups, were discovered in the open area.

attempt to protect herself from the ash and gas of the pyroclastic cloud (fig. 107).

Finally there was a group of four bodies discovered in the Vicolo degli Scheletri, used to make Giuseppe Fiorelli's first casts in 1863 and exhibited in the Antiquarium in Pompeii (fig. 108). This group consisted of a man, a woman, and two young girls, who were suffocated by the ash cloud as they attempted to escape the city, walking with difficulty over the thick layer of pumice. The woman fell on her back; near her earrings, a silver mirror and an amber pendant representing a Cupid were found. Trying to speed her flight, she probably had lifted up her garments, rolling them up to her stomach, a posture captured by the impression her body made. The man, who was holding some earrings and a key, had tried in vain to protect his head with a cape. The two young girls

107. Pompeii, Garden of the Fugitives, a group of human bodies discovered in 1961.

108. Pompeii, Antiquarium. Interior with casts of human bodies inside display cases (photo G. Sommer, late 1800s).

followed further back; one was knocked down on her side, and the other fell face down while she held a strip of fabric over her face.

ARRIA MARCELLA

The discovery that was mentioned more often than any other in nineteenth-century literature is one that was made on December 12, 1772, during the exploration of a large suburban building called the Villa of Diomedes (fig. 109). In a corridor of the cryptoporticus, twenty bodies were found buried within a layer of ash on the ancient ground level. The ash, having been compressed, took on the shape of the figures.

The discovery aroused great emotion in those who were participating in the excavations and then in visitors to the site. Indeed, it provided the first impetus for the development of romantic literature about the discovery of human bodies in ancient Pompeii. The cryptoporticus of the Villa, which had skylights to let in sunlight from the garden, had been used by the owner as a cellar for storing amphorae of wine, which were found leaning against the wall. It was next to these amphorae that 18 victims of the eruption were uncovered. Their bodies, confused and piled one atop another, were buried in the hardened ash; two more were found near the

109. Pompeii, Villa of Diomedes, porticoed garden (Anonymous, late nineteenth century, color lithograph).

121

entrance. These were identified immediately as the inhabitants of the Villa, the owner with his family and slaves (the latter recognizable by their poor garments). They had sought refuge in this place, which provided cover from the dense rain of pumice and lapilli, waiting with fear and trepidation for the eruptive fury to cease. But death struck them in the form of suffocation, due to the flows of ash around dawn on August 25, which easily penetrated through the skylights, despite the victims' futile attempts to shield their mouths with their clothing. Most of the victims also were wearing head coverings, which they had used earlier to protect themselves in some way from the pumice. One woman, in her final moments alive, covered her head with the hem of her garments, in a vain attempt to defend herself from the surge's mass of ash and gas; next to her skeleton, various pieces of gold jewelry were found. But the discovery that created the greatest sensation was the impression left in the ash of the body of a young woman. The excavators attempted to save at least part of this dramatic testimony of the eruption, and they managed to cut away from the bank of ash the impression of her breast and arms. This was brought to the *Reale Gabinetto di Portici* and then to the Archaeological Museum of Naples. On display, this became a destination for curiosity seekers of all types, attracted by the most emotional aspects of the rediscovery of Pompeii.

This same find, now so "famous" that it was admired by Théophile Gauthier during his trip to Italy in 1850, provided the writer with the inspiration for a romantic tale set in Pompeii. The story has two interpretations. The breast impressed in the fragment of ash is transformed into Arria Marcella, who, during a fantastical nocturnal visit to Pompeii, appears to the protagonist as the symbol of eternal beauty and "classicism," beyond worldly space (fig. 110). At the same time the young girl also became an emblem for pagan sensuality and joie de vivre, without ties and constrictions, in opposition to the oppressive and damaging Christian faith to which her father had converted: *Oh Arrio, father mine, do not oppress me in the name of this gloomy religion that was never mine; I believe in our ancient gods who loved life, youth, beauty, and pleasure.*

THE NUCERIAN GATE GROUP

Thus in the old man of the Nucerian Gate I saw the last mendicant of Pompeii, with his stick, knapsack, and bowl, which he had when he stopped beneath the porticoes of the Forum, in expectation of some coin or a scrap of meat and bread. But we have sought in vain in the knapsack and bowl for any trace of a coin. Having reached the banks of the Acheron, he did not have the most meager of offerings for the Charon's ferryboat. He was turned back into the infernal storm of ash, together with a throng of other fugitives.
With these words, Amedeo Maiuri, the great scholar of Pompeii, recorded the discovery of the body of an elderly man, outside the Nucerian Gate. Along with this victim, who fell amid the mausoleums of the

110. Pompeii, Via delle Tombe. Arria Marcella (Anonymous, late 1800s, lithograph).

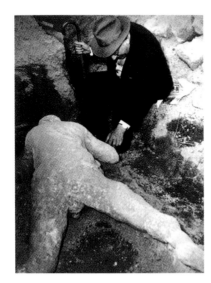

111a. Pompeii, Via Nocera necropolis. Amedeo Maiuri, looking at the cast made from a human body discovered in September 1956.

111b. Pompeii, the Nucerian Gate necropolis during excavation work.

monumental necropolis, three other bodies came to light (figs. 111 a–b). The first, an adult, face downward on the ground, was identified as a slave from a nearby house, due to the absence of any precious objects on his person. He had barely managed to get past the arches of the gateway when the dark whirlwinds that overtook him from behind forced him to turn off the road, in front of a wall. There he fell to the ground, exhausted, and suffocated. Two other fugitives, a man and a woman, were discovered between the gate and the first tower to the east. Perhaps after a desperate race over the pumice, they fell from the walls, which at that point were only a few meters high; they would have gotten as far as the first fields, but within a few meters the flow struck them, and they fell down, one next to the other.

Principal Eruptions of Vesuvius
from 25,000 Years Ago until 1631

Name of Eruption	Type of Eruption	Age (years ago or years B.C. or A.D.)
Codola	Plinian	25,000 years ago
Sarno	Plinian	22,000 years ago
Basal Pumice	Plinian	17,000 years ago
Pomici Verdoline (pale green pumice)	Plinian	15,500 years ago
Lagno Amendolare	Plinian	11,400 years ago
Mercato	Plinian	8,000 years ago
Avellino	Plinian	3,600 years ago
-	Sub-Plinian	1,200–1,400 B.C.
-	Sub-Plinian	800 B.C.
Pompeii	Plinian	A.D. 79
-	Explosive	A.D. 203
Pollena	Sub-Plinian	A.D. 472
-	Sub-Plinian ?	A.D. 512
-	Strong	A.D. 685
-	Large	A.D. 787
-	Strong	A.D. 968
-	Strong	A.D. 999
-	Strong	A.D. 1007
-	Large	A.D. 1037
-	Explosive	A.D. 1139
-	Phreatic explosion ?	A.D. 1500
-	Sub-Plinian	A.D. 1631

Principal Eruptions of Vesuvius in the Period 1631–1944

Beginning of eruption	Type of eruption	Notes
July 3, 1660	Explosive	Fall of ash toward NE
April 13, 1694	Effusive	Lava toward Torre del Greco
May 25, 1698	Effusive Explosive	Damage from fall of ash in Boscotrecase, Torre Annunziata, Ottaviano
July 28, 1707	Effusive Explosive	
May 20, 1737	Effusive Explosive	A lava flow invades T. del Greco; fall of ash and lahar
December 23, 1760	Effusive Explosive	Opening of lateral fissures on the S side (150 m slm); a lava flow toward T. Annunziata
October 19, 1767	Effusive Explosive	Two lava flows toward T. Torre Annunziata and S. Giorgio a Cremano
August 8, 1779	Explosive	Ash and volcanic ejects on Ottaviano
June 15, 1794	Effusive Explosive	Opening of fissures to SW (470 m slm); Lava flow toward T. del Greco
October 22, 1822	Effusive Explosive	Two lava flows toward T. del Greco and Boscotrecase
August 23, 1834	Effusive Explosive	Lava flow toward Poggiomarino
February 6, 1850	Effusive Explosive	
May 1, 1855	Effusive	Lava flow invades Massa and S. Sebastiano
December 8, 1861	Effusive Explosive	Opening of lateral fissures to SW (290 m slm)
April 24, 1872	Effusive Explosive	Lava flow invades Massa and S. Sebastiano
April 4, 1906	Effusive Explosive	Lava flow toward T. Annunziata, strong activity
June 3, 1929	Effusive Explosive	Lava flow toward Terzigno
March 18, 1944	Effusive Explosive	Lava flow invades Massa and S. Sebastiano

Glossary of Volcanology

CALDERA: A broad depression, volcanic in origin, generally circular in form, characterized by sub-vertical walls and a diameter greater than one kilometer; it is created when a section overlying the magmatic chamber collapses, and the chamber empties out in a violent eruption.

CRATER: Sub-circular depression located above the volcanic conduit, generally at the summit or along the sides of the volcanic edifice, through which the volcanic material is emitted.

ERUPTION: Expulsion, often violent, of fused, solid, or gaseous volcanic material from the crater, following the rise of magma in the volcanic conduit.

FALLOUT: The eruptive phase characterized by the fall of pyroclastic materials from the eruptive cloud.

LAHAR (MUD FLOW): Rapid movement of pyroclastic material, previously deposited along the sides of the volcano and saturated with rainwater, that flows downhill, generally stopping at the foot of the slopes.

LAPILLI: Pyroclastic fragments, between 2 and 64 mm in size, ejected during an explosive eruption.

LAVA: Magma ejected onto the surface; the term is also used to indicate the rock formed after the magma has cooled down.

LAVA FOUNTAIN: Violent jets of magma that reach considerable heights from the mouth of the volcano (sometimes hundreds of meters), due to the pressure of gases that have been unleashed.

MAGMA: Material derived from the fusion of rock at high temperatures (generally between 900 and 1200° C / 1652–2192 °F), siliceous in composition, in which gases and solid crystalline fragments are present.

MAGMATIC CHAMBER: Zone where magma accumulates below the surface of the earth; the magma can remain motionless for long periods of time before rising through the volcanic conduit and reaching the surface, creating an eruption.

PAROXYSM: Violent phase of an explosive eruption.

PISOLITE: Volcanic products formed from the aggregation of fine material around a core of condensation.

PLINIAN: Strong explosive eruption similar to that of Vesuvius in A.D. 79, described by Pliny the Elder (hence the name) in two letters to Tacitus.

PROJECTILES: Pyroclastic material ejected from a volcano during an eruption.

PUMICE: Light, effusive rock, generally light gray in color, vitreous and very porous because of a multitude of air spaces, caused by the expansion of gas inside the magma and the subsequent rapid cooling; depending on the size, there can be pumice bombs (over 64 mm), pumice lapilli (2–64 mm), or ash (less than 2 mm).

PYROCLASTIC FLOW: Cloud made up of gases and solid fragments, with highly concentrated particles, characterized by high temperature and velocity, caused by the collapse of the eruptive column; the flows tend to run along the ground, pulled along by gravity; their paths are affected by the pre-existing morphology, pouring into valleys and filling depressions.

PYROCLASTITES: Volcanic rocks formed from pyroclasts.

PYROCLASTS (TEPHRA): Solid volcanic material such as ash, sand, lapilli, blocks, and volcanic bombs, ejected during an explosive eruption.

STRATOVOLCANO: Volcano made up of alternating lava and pyroclastic layers.

SURGE (BASE-SURGE): Turbulent cloud made up of gas and solid fragments, with a low concentration of particles, characterized by high temperature and velocity; surges generally are associated with phreatomagmatic eruptions and form expansive, highly mobile clouds that run along the ground, dispersing over the preexisting topography.

VOLCANIC ASH: Fine volcanic material, less than 2 mm in size, produced during an eruption.

VOLCANIC BOMB: Magma fragment larger than 64 mm, expelled, still partially fused, during a volcanic explosion, according to a ballistic trajectory.

VOLCANIC CONDUIT: Pipelike or fissure-shaped opening, through which the magma rises to the surface.

VOLCANIC DOME: Dome-shaped swelling of the volcanic edifice, caused by an expulsion and accumulation of very viscous lava piling up near the center of emission.

VOLCANIC EXPLOSIONS: Violent emission of pyroclasts, due to the sudden liberation of gas from the magma.

Selected Bibliography

Albore, Livadie C.; D'Alessio, G.; Mastrolorenzo G.; Rolandi G. "Le eruzioni del Somma in epoca protostorica," in *Tremblements de terre, éruptions volcaniques et vie des hommes dans la Campanie antique*, Naples, 1986.

Archaologie und Seismologie, Colloquium Boscoreale 26-27/11/1993, Munich, 1995.

Bonifacio, G.; Sodo, A.M. *Stabiae. Guida archeologica alle ville*, Castellammare di Stabia, 2001.

Bulwer-Lytton, E.G. *Gli ultimi giorni di Pompei* (trans. by F. Cusani), Milan, 1835.

Capasso, L. *I fuggiaschi di Ercolano Paleo-biologia delle vittime dell'eruzione vesuviana del 79 d.C.*, Rome, 2001.

Casali di ieri-Casali di oggi, architetture rurali e tecniche agricole nel territorio di Pompei e Stabiae, Naples, 2000.

Ciarallo, A. *Verde pompeiano*, Rome, 2000.

Cioni, R.; Marianelli, P.; Sbrana, A. "L'eruzione del 79 d.C: stratigrafia dei depositi ed impatto sugli insediamenti romani nel settore orientale e meridionale del Somma-Vesuvio, in *Rivista di Studi Pompeiani*, IV, 1992.

Cortini, M.; Scandone, R. *Un'introduzione alla vulcanologia, Magmi Eruzioni Vulcani*, Naples, 1987.

De Carolis, E. "Testimonianze archeologiche in area vesuviana posteriori al 79 d.C." in *Archeologia Uomo Territorio*, 16, 1987.

De Carolis, E.; Groppelli, G. "Nuove ipotesi sul seppellimento di Ercolano (Napoli): prospettive dall'integrazione di dati archeologici e vulcanologici," *Archeologia Uomo Territorio*, 18, 1999.

De Carolis, E.; Patricelli, G.; Ciarallo, A. "Rinvenimenti di corpi umani nell'area urbana di Pompei," in *Rivista di Studi Pompeiani*, IX, 1998 (2000).

De Carolis, E. *Pompei. Itinerario archeologico ragionato*, Portici, 2000.

Fergola, L.; Pagano, M. *Oplontis. Itinerario archeologico ragionato*, Portici, 1999.

Gasparini, P.; Musella, S. *Un viaggio al Vesuvio*, Naples, 1991.

Guadagno, G. "Il viaggio di Plinio il Vecchio verso la morte (Plin. Ep., VI, 16) in *Rivista di Studi Pompeiani*, VI, 1993-1994 (1996).

Nazzaro, A. *Il Vesuvio: storia eruttiva e teorie vulcanologiche*, Naples, 1997.

Pagano, M. *Ercolano. Itinerario archeologico ragionato*, Portici, 1998.

Patricelli, G. "I fenomeni premonitori delle grandi eruzioni esplosive," Experimental Degree Thesis in Geophysics, presented March 26, 1996 (delivered by Prof. P. Gasparini), University of Naples Federico II, Faculty of Geological Sciences.

Patricelli, G.; De Carolis, E. "L'eruzione del Vesuvio del 79 d.C.: le vittime dell'antica Pompei," in *Atti del III e IV ciclo di conferenze di geologia, storia e archeologia* (ed. F. Senatore), Pompeii, January 1999–May 2000, Rome, 2001.

Pescatore, T.; Sigurdsson, H. "L'eruzione del Vesuvio del 79 d.C.," in *Ercolano 1738-1988. 250 anni di ricerca archeologica*, Rome, 1993.

Pescatore, T.; Senatore, M.R.; Capretto, G.; Lerro, G.; Patricelli, G. "Ricostruzione paleoambientale delle aree circostanti l'antica città di Pompei (Campania, Italia) al tempo dell'eruzione del Vesuvio del 79 d.C.," in *Bollettino Società Geologica Italiana*, 118 (1999).

Pesce, Al; Rolandi, G. *Vesuvio 1944, l'ultima eruzione*, San Sebastiano, 1994.

Sigurdsson, H.; Carey, S.; Cornell, W., Pescatore, T. "The eruption of Vesuvius in A.D. 79," in *National Geographic Research*, I, 1985.

Storie da un'eruzione. Pompei Ercolano Oplontis, Milano 2003.

Varone, A. *Pompei. I misteri di una città sepolta*, Rome, 2000.

Index

Page references to illustrations are in italic.

Printed in Rome May 2003
«L'ERMA» di BRETSCHNEIDER
by Tipograf S.r.l.
via Costantino Morin, 26/A